Ben-ti-hon

Blar-neala

Loch Turret

Glen

Falls

Invergeldy

Daden

Nether Invergeldy

Cashvackchen

Crosswhennel

W.Fentalich

E.Fentalich

Balnacoul

Ballachallach

Finasha

Carn-u-lowse

MONIVAIR

Carrcolen

Lurg

Batimeanoch

Tynacroy

G.ashlarich

Kenaguar

Lurg

W.Balmack

E.Balma

Glascarry

Babnemeanoch

Corry

Craigvayne

Devils Caldron

T

R

A

Dru

Daniera

Gerrichrow

W.Crapoch

Movy

Belna

E.Crapoch

Mid

Dalhonvie

Ballinlochin

Balichfoich

Tullyvanochle

Baliniuig

W.Tullivano

cher

Lawers House

Balinlug

Brinichrow

Clathic

E.Clathic

Quing

Millown

Lawers

Woodside

Mains

Carse

Thor

Rechterscallan

Ross

Comrie

Fichterscallan

W.Dalginross

E.Dalginross

Lennoch

Carse

Blackford

Aberuchill

Craigish

Blairdrich

Roman

Camp

Faurnes

Movrend

Drummond-

er-noch

Cowden

STROWAN

Renecroy

Cuilt

Walranich

Green Burnt

Ruchillside

Guildrach

Dalchetel

Mill of

Fortline

Glentin

Achnagarrick

Grefurry

Carse

Drumachure

Newtown

Croitechrost

Milutime

W.shaer Litt.Mill

Trean

E.Miger

Glashnased

Straid

Cragneich

Blar

more

Dalness

Malter-more

Cullory

Crutack

Millown

PART OF

MONIVAIRD

RUACHILL Water

RTVEY

David B. McNaughton

UPPER STRATHEARN
From Earliest times to today

A Study of its Places and People

A

The line drawings are by my son-in-law, Norman Aiton of Muthill.

Sincere thanks are due to the John Jamieson Munro Charitable Trust and its administrators without whose help this book could not have been published.

Published by Jamieson & Munro

Printed by Sunprint, 36 Tay Street, Perth and 40 Craigs, Stirling.

ISBN: 0 9500647 4 2

I offer this book to my long-suffering wife with love, and as a token of thanks for her tholing many long hours of my rather inadequate typing.

The author in Glenartney. View overlooking village of Comrie and Upper Strathearn.

TABLE OF CONTENTS

A WORD TO THE READER

This book does not set out to be an exhaustive history of Upper Strathearn. It is rather a series of essays or writings on a variety of places and persons which together encompass much of its story.

My intention in setting down this information has been partly, because I am greatly interested in local history and in the background of ordinary folk, but rather more to try to satisfy the endless questionings of people, often from distant places, who have come to make their homes here. They are very curious about the past, and sadly, because they just do not know, they pass by many places and things which would be of interest to them. They have come here because they have admired the beauties of the surroundings, and perhaps, only knowing that Comrie, for instance, is the village with the mirror at an awkward corner, or that it is the home of Scottish earthquakes, and not much else. As they enquire a bit more deeply, they find that the strath is a place of many surprises and endless interest.

Not much has been put into print about Strathearn for many years, and such writing as there is is long out of print. I feel, therefore, that it will not be amiss to set down the thoughts of a native whose reading over the years has been extensive, and whose researches have ranged far beyond to archives in Edinburgh and elsewhere. It has seemed good to me to bring much of that lore together, and my hope is that this small book will be of interest and pleasure to newcomers, to visitors who increasingly come here, and even, to many whose lives have been spent here.

I have found, too, while writing this book, that many folk abroad, particularly in Canada and The States, though they are long gone from this place, almost two hundred years in some cases, they have a hankering to know something of the history of their forefathers' birthplace. Much correspondence with these "cousins abroad", and meetings, both here and across the Atlantic, have shown me that, as our story is also their story, I should make some attempt to incorporate them in this book. This I have done.

I wish to express my sincere thanks to several friends who over the past few years have assisted me in the gathering of information, particularly to Bill Gardiner whose background knowledge is profound, to Jim Mitchell who has provided the illustrations either first-hand or by reproduction from old photographs, and especially to Mrs Agnes Watt who has been a source of inspiration and encouragement. All three are natives of Comrie and share my love and enthusiasm for the place. I owe, too, a debt of gratitude for help in typing the work in its early form to my daughter, Christine Aiton and for final typing and beautiful layout to Ginette Morin of Montreal, Canada.

FOREWORD

Among the fair straths of Scotland there are few which can equal and none surpass in beauty the Strath of Earn, at least in its upper reaches. What the geologic ages have formed, the hand of man has softened and made more lovely. Mountain and hill, river and stream, woodland and meadow, all combine in a harmonious whole to satisfy the eye and to pleasure the heart and mind. The very seasons of the year, with their ever-changing variety, serve, each in its due time, to make more beautiful what nature and man have together created and contrived.

At the heart of Upper Strathearn lie the village and parish of Comrie, and the adjoining parishes of Muthill, Monzievaird and Strowan, and Balquhidder. Between them they contain most of the glory of the strath. Farther downstream, below the junction of the Earn and Turret, there is much that is fair and lovely, but here the Earn has grown aged and broadened her valley; the mountains have receded and the hills become rolling undulations. The speed and sparkle have gone from the water and the grandeur of the upper strath has given way to pastoral peace and quietude. Here, in more tractable soils and levels, improving agriculture has made a fair and pleasant land, rich in crops and herds, rewarding enough in their own way to the eye, but lacking the sheer beauty and surprise which greet one at every turn of the road west of Crieff.

It is my purpose to treat especially of the Parish of Comrie, but one cannot do so in isolation as to time and space. It will be necessary to cross parish boundaries and travel even further afield, for much that happened in one place had its effect on another. We shall, therefore, consider what were the influences which made the district as we know it today. Long ages of time before the written record of history, several thousand years, evidenced by a few mere isolated groups of stones and burial mounds, tell us the story, until we can pick up the thin thread of more reliable information from the pens or stili of ancient Rome. Our evidence henceforward lies in the writings of long-dead clerics from Ireland or Scotia, and ancient Alban, in legal dispositions of Celtic and Anglo-Norman overlords of ancient times, who themselves could neither read nor write. Their wills and intentions are set down for us by clerics, until a brighter light shines in Stuart times, and we no longer have to peer darkly and guess between the lines, but we find our story written for all to read; and no longer do we have to rely on dimly-remembered folk-history, albeit, more and more of which is now shown to be founded on truth and to have been carried down with careful accuracy.

We shall therefore, look at these influences in their time-order and try to see how it comes about that our beautiful valley came to acquire its varied shapes and features; why it is that our lochs, rivers and streams were born and grew to lusty life; why it is that our mountains and hills are constituted as they are; whence came our deep receding glens and peat-moss haggs, our ravines and waterfalls, our slatey hillsides and our level fields laid on deep gravels.

Much, much later, came the first man, probing with uncertain steps until he found that here he could have some surety of living, that here there was a sufficiency of game, fish, fowl and flesh, to supply the wants of his family, without the need to range too widely. There would not have been many of his kind, perhaps but a few dozens at first. Here, hemmed in by the hills, woods and marshes, he could go about providing for his own, without too much danger from others of his own kind. In time, his descendants would learn and begin to practise the simple crafts of raising grains and domesticating small herds and flocks. They would grow in number and become associated with other families, albeit loosely, until we have the first recognizably named peoples, the Caledonians, who came into collision with the might of Rome and her legions. If Rome's direct influence on them was fleeting and merely that of a more powerful and more disciplined adversary, at least it serves to put our ancestors upon the written pages of history.

In course of time, at least some of these so-called Caledonii became the Picts of Alban. The Picts formed seven confederations or kingdoms in Alban, and of these, one between the Forth and the Tay, was Fortrenn or Fortriu, comprising the districts we now know as Menteith and Strathearn, with their capital at Forteviot and with one of their strongholds at Dundurn, (Dun Duirn) just east of Loch Earn, the Fort of the Fist. The name may come from the dour, stubborn, close-knit shape of the eminence. Here, over the centuries, they engaged in battle with those other peoples of the original Celtic stock, the Scoti of Dalriada, and with whom they eventually merged long afterwards to form the beginnings of the kingdom we now know as Scotland.

During this period, the still few inhabitants of Strathearn, who may well have been much more numerous than we, at times, think, had progressed from being mere hunters of beasts and birds to being pastoralists and primitive cultivators of the soil. They had passed far along the road to modernity. They had tamed the wild auroch of the woods to provide them with sustenance and aid in their labours, and the dog was their constant companion for hunting and herding. They had achieved a settled mode of life and in the manner of such settled communities, had chosen to live under the rule of such primitive law as, with the

Foreword

advancing years, they found desirable for life together in reasonable harmony. And as with any community of men, certain showed qualities of leadership above the ordinary, and these they chose to be their chiefs. Some of the names are known to us from Classical writers and such sources as the Chronicles of the Picts and Scots, but others have no known memorial than such works of their hands as have withstood the vagaries of time, and these are few.

With the decline of the old Pictish kingdoms and the emergence, more or less, of what is now the kingdom of Scotland, part of the kingdom of Fortrenn became the Celtic Earldom of Strathearn, subject in part to the old customary rules and laws of the Celts, and in part to the more formal, feudal laws imposed by men whose tenure owed much to kings imbued with the spirit of the Norman kings of England, and such barons as had, by one means or another, achieved a measure of possession in this part of Scotland.

It is now that we enter into what should be a period of easy decipherment and record. We now have deeds and charters, laws written and judgments delivered and set down, histories written and records kept, but, many of these are traps for the unwary, for men were aye 'kittle cattle', and no two witnesses ever seem to see the facts of the same incident in the same light. So many men have axes to grind and interests to serve and, indeed, truth lies at the bottom of a deep, deep well. It has been truly said that a Scotsman's worst enemy is another Scot, and that he need look no further than his nearest neighbour for trouble. The sword and the dirk lay ever ready to our grip and little provocation called them from their sheaths. This feuding propensity has clouded our past and has often been carried over into our written records, falsifying facts and distorting what should have been clear, often long years afterwards, to bolster otherwise shaky rights and claims. A way through these tortuous morasses is hard to see and the truth difficult to find.

CHAPTER I

EARLY HISTORY·
OF COMRIE AND UPPER STRATHEARN

Much of what Comrie folk think of as Comrie, does not lie in Comrie Parish at all. Much of Glenlednock is in Monzievaird and Strowan, much of Glenartney is in Muthill and there is a very curious small enclave which lies in Monzievaird. It is difficult at this late stage to decide why these divisions are so. They go back a very long way to the days of the Mediaeval Church and had to do with the locations of churches and priests. I am of opinion that many lines were so drawn because of the poorness of communications; the lack of proper roads; the lack of bridges. Resort had to be had to treacherous and changeable fords over the river.

I have not been able to trace the place-name, Comrie, as a written name, further back than the year 1268. There is little doubt that the name existed for a very long time before that as a descriptive name for "the coming together of the waters". Gaelic place-names almost always describe what one sees at the spot, and no place could be more appropriately named than Comrie. In the year 1268 the Celtic Earl of Strathearn, Earl Malise, granted a sum of money to the monks of the Abbey of Inchaffray, Insula Missarum, and as witnesses we find "dominis G J et B rectoribus ecclesiarum de Comry de Buchfydir (Balquhidder) de Monyhge (Monzie)".

The position of Comrie is unique, lying as it does on the Highland Boundary Fault running from Stonehaven to Helensburgh. Eastwards the land opens out into Lower Strathearn and the great Vale of Strathmore. Westwards we enter the narrow passes and defiles leading to the Highlands. It is not for nothing that Crieff, the first and nearest Lowland town has been called "the hangin' toon". Many a poor cateran has been led eastwards down Glenartney or by Loch Earn to kick his last on the "kindly gallows" of Crieff.

From earliest times our strath has seen war and bloodshed. The Romans have left their mark in the great camps of Dalginross, any trace of which is now lost except to the spade of the archaeologist or the eye of the aerial camera. The Scots of Dalriada penetrated down Glendochart and Loch Earn, the Danes sailed up the Tay, and the Northumbrians came over the Ochill passes. The local powerful families were a rapacious bunch, the Drummonds, the Murrays, the Campbells and the Stewarts, while the neighbouring small clans were not to be outdone in murder and rapine. Life here for the first 17 hundred years of the Christian Era must have been "nasty, brutish and short".

And who were the first folk to have their habitation here? They have no name, other than Neolithic, or New Stone Age Man. They must have been very numerous as the remaining works of their hands show. How much more should we have seen had we lived two hundred years ago, before the "improving" hand of agriculture removed so much! A glance at the map will show, too often, the legend, "site of standing stones", or "supposed tumulus". Still evident, though in diminished form, are a dozen or more standing stones, some the remnants of complete circles, the likely remains of a hut circle at Drum na Cille, with a very fine cup-marked stone in the near vicinity, and the ruins of a stone circle, bull-dozed aside within the past few years. The somewhat delapidated, I almost said, desecrated, burial at Kindrochat, and the still extant burial mounds at Ruchillside, which, we have been told, may be all that remains of a once great Neolithic cemetery.

Then, too, there is Dun Mhoid, the Mound of Judgement, by the cemetery wall and the intriguing "Castell Dun Dalig" near the Roman Camp, shown on an 18th. century drawing of the area. Could this be the same as the "Dalginross Court Knowe" of Farquharson's map of 1767?

In the year 79, Agricola invaded Scotland and, after a winter of preparation, advanced north in 80. Crossing the Forth at Stirling, he marched through Strathallan and entered Strathearn. He established his permanent camp at Ardoch and made an important temporary camp at Dalginross. He appears to have overrun the country as far as the Firth of Tay and we can still trace his camps at Bochastle, Fendoch and Strageath and along the Gask Ridge to Perth, with signal stations at intervals along the way. The tribes inhabiting our strath were the Verturiones, more generally called the Caledonians.

Some 250 years later, we find that the Caledonians are now called Picts, who, in alliance first with the Scots who had come from Ireland to Galloway and Argyll, began a continuing series of raids into Roman-held territory to the south. Finally, the Romans withdrew from Britain in 410 AD.

The Picts were now in process of setting themselves up into a series of seven kingdoms, of which Fortrenn, or more correctly, Fortriu, was one, the country between the rivers Forth and Tay, and even further north to the Mounth. Their capital was at Forteviot and one of their chief strongholds was at Dundurn, "The Fort of the Fist" now sometimes called St. Fillan's Hill. They were converted to Christianity about the year 556 by missionary monks from Iona. There followed much conflict in Strathearn, battles with the encroaching Scots from Dalriada in Argyllshire and with the Northumbrians from the south east invading through the passes of the Ochills. Finally, about the year 843, the Picts and Scots united under Kenneth II, Kenneth Macalpine and formed the Kingdom of Alban, later

3

Scotland.

It is from now that we learn of the rise to power of the Celtic Earls of Atholl, Menteith and Strathearn. The boundaries of the ancient Earldom of Strathearn enclosed an immense tract of the country; in the east from Newburgh near the junction of the Earn with the Tay estuary, in the west the western bounds of the Braes of Balquhidder, the Grampians in the north and the Ochills in the south. Within these limits, the old earls exercised almost kingly powers, and their authority was immense. They are known to us by their first names only, as family names did not arise in Britain before the Norman Conquest. Not much of their early history is known but that they had positions of power and authority from early times is certain. They were among the foremost leaders of the Celtic party in Scotland and strove manfully to uphold their native customs against the innovations of David I and his Saxon and Norman chivalry, for these latter had spread widely over Scotland within the first century of the Norman Conquest of England.

Malise, Earl of Strathearn, fought in the great Scots army which invaded England in 1138 under David I and met overwhelming defeat in the Battle of the Standard. Malise was one of the five hostages given to England for the preservation of peace.

The next Earl, Ferteth, headed a conspiracy of native Scots in 1160 against the English councils of Malcom IV, and attempted to seize the king. They were fought off, but so powerful were they that they could not be made to answer for their actions and, through the good offices of the Church, became reconciled to the King. Ferteth's son, Earl Gilbert, followed Norman fashions and took charters for his lands and connected himself with Norman families through marriages. Like David I, "ane soir sanct for the Crown", Earl Gilbert made great gifts to the Church, and particularly to the Abbey of Inchaffray, the Isle of the Masses, which he had founded as an Augustinian house in the year 1200. His eldest son was buried within the Abbey, which, near Madderty, is now but a tumbled heap of stones. One of the strongholds of the family was Tom a Chasteil, the eminence on which stands the monument to Sir David Baird at Monzievaird.

Scotland was now becoming more and more exposed to the feudalising influences of the King, particularly of King David and his Norman favourites from England. It is from now that we see a gradual swing of the balance in favour of the hard, logical, legalistic rule of the Normans, away from the kindlier, more artistic, paternalistic and family-based way of life of the Celts. We have records of eight Celtic Earls of Strathearn of whom the last was Malise V, born in 1315. He resigned the earldom into the hands of Baliol, and the earldom came into the King's gift--where it still remains. It is reserved to the Royal Family. The last to hold the title was the Duke of Connaught; Queen Victoria's father was Duke of Kent and Strathearn.

Before finally reverting to the Crown, the Earldom passed through several lay hands. There was a Moray Earl--Sir John Moray of Drumsergard. He was followed by Robert, High Steward of Scotland, nephew of King David II. When Robert became king in 1370, as Robert II, he bestowed the earldom on his son David and it was at this time that the earldom became a Palatinate, which, in essence, means that the Earl could exercise almost the same powers as Royalty. Hereafter the earldom was bestowed on the family of Graham, the last earl being Malise Graham who was deprived of his title by James I who coveted the rich lands of Strathearn. James I was murdered in the Blackfriars' Monastery at Perth in February 1437. One of the chief conspirators and assassins was Sir Robert Graham, uncle of Malise.

It is about this time that we first hear of the Drummond family in Strathearn. They trace their descent from one, Maurice, a Hungarian, who came over with the Saxon princess Margaret from her exile in Hungary

5

after the Norman invasion of England. She, of course, married Malcolm Canmore, and in time became known as St. Margaret of Scotland for her beneficence to the church. The Drummonds were well rewarded for their services and became great landowners in the Lennox and Stirlingshire. It is, in all probability, from Drymen in Stirlingshire that they take their name. They became Stewards of Strathearn and Keepers of the King's Forests. In 1491, Sir John Drummond was given a licence by James IV to build the castle of Drummond at Concraig, near Muthill. Devoted followers of the Stuarts, the Drummonds were twice attainted and their estates forfeited in the '15 and '45, to be finally restored to the family in 1797. The lands and titles henceforward came by marriage to the family of Ancaster, the Willoughby de Eresbys.

Comrie from monument.

CHAPTER II

STONE AGE AND ROMAN REMAINS

With the melting of the great ice sheets at the close of the last Ice Age, some 9 or 10 thousand years ago, the face of Scotland must have been bare and bleak, almost beyond our understanding. The grinding action of the ice as it flowed across the land would not only have planed down the mountain tops and gouged out lochs and river channels, but would have removed all vestiges of life, both plant and animal. Though the ice had gone the environment would remain uninviting and hostile for many centuries to come. The earliest hesistant comers must have arrived along the coasts, finding shelter in caves on the raised beaches where they could sustain themselves on shell fish and such fish as they could catch with their primitive harpoons and hooks. The evidence for this lies in the mounds of discarded shells and simple artefacts at various points along our coasts. It would be a long age before they ventured far from the sea.

One can only guess when man first arrived in Strathearn and whether he came from the west from Argyll or from the east up the valley of the Earn, possibly the latter, as this would make for an easier journey by water. In the absence of primitive weapons or tools as evidence it does not seem likely that any of the Stone Age peoples came here even though a competent young archaeologist has told us that the tumuli remaining at Ruchillside are part of a great Neolithic cemetery. Without skilled excavation it is impossible to tell. We can merely surmise.

We can state with some certainty that in the Bronze and Iron Ages, Comrie district was fairly populous as the many standing stones and remains of stone circles bear witness. It has been estimated that within five miles from the centre of the village there are some nineteen sites. There may well be many others which so far have not come to light or of which merely some small traces remain. We know, for example, of two stone circles in the fields opposite Old Craggish which were both destroyed about 1891 and were incorporated in the structure of the new Craggish farmhouse, itself but recently demolished. At Tullibannocher below the Crappich Hills are two stones where once there were four forming a circle. A local farmer reported that at the end of the nineteenth century there had been but three stones remaining and as one, which had fallen, hindered the working of the plough, it too, had been removed. Within our own times, some ten years ago, a circle of stones at Drumnakeil was bulldozed aside on the instructions of the then landowner and pushed into a ditch. Among them was a large cup-marked boulder with thirteen beautifully clear-cut cups. Fortunately, this boulder has been left in a position where one can examine the cup-marks without difficulty. We can only regret that 'improving' agriculture and downright vandalism have removed so much of the evidence of early man in Strathearn.

On the farm of Kindrochet, on the south bank of the Earn some two miles from St. Fillans, lies a much desecrated burial mound. This must have been opened some time in the 19th. century and again was closely examined by Professor Gordon Childe around 1930. The cairn stones lie scattered about and the remnants of stone cists are exposed. Field stones have been dumped on the site and even an electricity pylon has been sited there. So much for conservation!

At Drumnakeil, as already mentioned, some 400 feet above Kindrochat and within mutual sight, is a roughly oval site which we have been told may be the remains of a hut circle. The site is flat and the remains of the walls, if that is what they were, still stand to a height of about 4 feet. Just east of this structure was the site of the now demolished stone circle. There is a strange tradition that here was the burial place of "wee, unchristened bairns" whose remains were often brought long distances, from as far away as Killin, for example. Certainly, the name Drumnakeil means Chapel Ridge and there may well have been some sort of religious structure here. Not far away, leading into Glenlednock is a pass in the hills named Beallach an t-Sagairt, the Priest's Pass.

The most obvious standing stone in our locality lies on Dalginross Moor just at the entrance roadway to Cowden Farm. It is an irregularly shaped stone of considerable weight and alongside are two smaller stones, the middle one may well be an interloper, while the other has incised upon it some 22 neatly made cups. The site is right on the southern edge of the Roman marching camp and would thus have been well-known to the invaders.

About one half mile to the east of these stones, is what, today, may be called a four-poster, consisting of two upright and two recumbent stones. They lie at the north-east corner of the cemetery and have the name Dunmhoid, the Mound of Judgment. According to a report by the parish minister of the time, the Rev. John Macpherson, some excavation was carried out and a stone cist was revealed containing a thigh-bone.

In a field near the Crieff to Comrie road, in front of the mansion house of Lawers, stands a whinstone monolith of close on six feet in height.

All of the foregoing stones lie in the flat river plain of the Earn save for those at Drumnakeil.

The Blairnroar and Dunruchan districts are rich in standing stones. Many can be seen in the distance from the Comrie to Braco road as one passes Middleton

Farm. It has been supposed that these were set up by the Romans as guideposts for troops marching from Ardoch Camp to that at Dalginross. This seems highly unlikely as the Romans never erected other than dressed and inscribed stones. We may be confident that they are the work of early man in the district. The great stone in the yard at Auchingarrich Farm and that at Craigneich are within easy access. The others lie away out on the moor.

The tumuli at Ruchillside, now Cultibraggan Farm, probably date from the second millenium B.C. Three of these do not appear to have undergone any examination, though tree-planting had been done on them, probably in the 19th. century, but a fourth has been ploughed down to the field level and merely shows as a circle in the crops.

The rocky outcrop west of the parish church is traditionally the site of ancient stones which were probably removed when the first Free Church was built in 1843, and may be built into it. The Knoll is named Tom a Chessaig and St. Kessock is said to have preached here.

About one mile from St. Fillans, rising abruptly from the level plain, stands St. Fillan's Hill. This eminence has a double significance. In Pictish days it was a strong fortress of the kings of Fortrenn under the name of Dundurn, or The Fort of the Fist. The rock rises steeply from all sides and in the days of its pride, in addition to its natural defences, had great walls of stones. These must have been carried up from the river level and the labour involved must have been immense as the great screes of fallen stones weigh many thousands of tons. Doubtless, Dundurn suffered from assault by the encroaching Scots from Dalriada. The Pictish king, King Girig or Grig was slain here in 878 when is recorded, "mortuus est in Dundeorn".

It was here, too, in 520 that the Celtic monk St. Fillan, the Leper, or Stammerer brought Christianity from Ireland to the Picts of Fortrenn. At the highest point of the rock is a naturally shaped stone seat from which the Saint is said to have preached. Here, too, was a holy well which for centuries in the days of the early Church was frequented by persons seeking relief from a great variety of ills. Even as late as 1791 no fewer than 70 persons visited the well seeking cure for sore eyes, barrenness, and rheumatism. The remedy for the last seems drastic as the invalid "must ascend the hill, sit in this chair, then lie down on their back, and be pulled by the legs to the bottom of the hill." An early form of traction, no doubt!

It should be noted that this St. Fillan, called of Rathearn, who flourished in the early 6th. century should not be confused with the St. Fillan of Glendochart who died in the year 749. It was this saint's arm-bone which gave comfort and encouragement to Robert Bruce before the Battle of Bannockburn, and whose Quigrich, or pastoral staff, is such a glorious possession of the Scottish people in the care of the Museum of Scots Antiquities in Edinburgh.

Though little is today to be seen of the Roman Marching Camp of Dalginross or of its two small attendant fortlets, it was of strategic importance to Agricola when he moved east in Strathearn to Perth and beyond, to his great victory at Mons Graupius. Its extent is such that it would have contained a weak legion and guarded the outlets from the west by Loch Earn. Might it be that Dalginross is described by the Roman geographer, Strabo, as "last, loneliest, loveliest, exquisite, apart", the utmost outpost of the Roman Empire, and one of the boundaries of the habitable globe? One can imagine the awe and trepidation which must have entered the hearts of even the hardiest of Roman soldiers when they crossed from the Central Lowlands into full view of the Highland Hills and glens rising before them, well-knowing that here was the homeland of warrior tribes who stood not in awe of the might of Rome. The Roman incursion was not of long duration and though they returned again a hundred years later, they preferred to lie quiet behind the ramparts of Hadrian's Wall among the docile, subdued tribes of the south.

These remains, few in number, yet serve to link us to our earliest ancestors, to the great days of Rome, and to the earliest burgeoning of Christianity in these islands, save the earlier missionary work of St. Ninian of Whithorn and his followers.

St Fillans Hill or Dundurn, a Pictish stronghold. Here St Fillan preached and King Girig was slain.

CHAPTER III

THE TIME OF THE BISHOPS

From 1662 to 1688, that is from the Restoration of Charles II to the coming of William III, the Parish of Comrie was under the Kirk Jurisdiction of the Diocese of Dunblane, whose first Bishop during the "Time of the Bishops" was Robert Leighton, a fair-minded and easy-going prelate, very unlike his brother Archbishop Sharp of St. Andrews, who was later murdered on Magus Muir on 3rd. May, 1679.

It will be noted that the system of Kirk Government was a mixture of Diocesan Synods and Presbyteries. Moderators of Presbyteries formed with the Bishop and his Episcopal officers the Synodical body. It was a mix of Presbyterianism and Episcopalianism.

The Register of the Diocesan Synod of Dunblane casts many sidelights on the social conditions of the times, which directly or indirectly affected the life of the folk of Comrie Parish. Generally, in the Diocese under the wise and fairly lenient bishops, Leighton and his successors, the people conformed to Episcopal rule. Even so, we have indications that some of the compulsory methods applied in other districts to enforce regularity in observing religious observances, had their effect here.

"April 28, 1663. Enacted that the Readers at kirks doe keep a register of burials, as well as of Baptisms and Marriages." Doubtless this enactment was put into force, but the earliest extant records of baptisms for Comrie date only from 1693; henceforward they appear to have been fairly kept, but with many gaps and inaccuracies. Much depended upon the attitudes of Ministers and Session Clerks. There were few places in life into which the Kirk did not enter, as will be seen from the following extracts.

"Whereas in times past there has been two bursars keepit by the two respective Presbyteries (i.e. Auchterarder and Dunblane) at the study of divinity, and the maintenance for that end being but small so that it could not sustene them constantlie thereat three-quarters of a year--it is enacted by the Bishop and Synod that there shall be but one bursar in tyme to come keepit by the two Presbyteries at the foresaid college (St. Andrews), who is to have ane hundred pounds Scottis for his maintenance yearlie; quhilk sum is to be paid at his entrie to the college. The quhilk bursar is to be nominate by the Bishop himself, and lykwys the bursar is obliged to remain constantlie three quarters completelie everie year during his abode thereat."

"April 13th. 1664. The quhilk day, William Low, ane poor man in the parish of Kincardine, who had his house and goods therein consumed by fire, presented ane supplicatioune desyring some supplie. The Bishop and Synod, taking the poor man his cause to their serious consideratioune, did refer him to the several kirkes within the Diocese for some supplie."

Mr Row was minister at Monzievaird in 1655 as successor to Mr William Weemys. In 1661 a grant was made to him of £50 by Parliament on account of the sufferings he had undergone in supporting the royal cause.

"Aprill, 1665, James Row, minister of Monzievaird and Strowan, declared 'that there should be but one kirk for them both, and that to be built in a place more convenient between the two paroches'."

"October 10th. 1665. Recommended to the brethren of Ochterardore Presbytery to appoint ane day for visiting and perambulating the bounds of Monivaird and Strowan, anent the building of ane chuch in a more convenient place than now it is for the present, for the benefit of the two united parishes."

"October 11th. 1665. Recommended to the presbytery of Ochterardore to speak with the heritors of the parish of Comrie, and especiallie with the Earle cf Perth, anent the speedie provyding of the kirk of Comrie with a minister." The perambulation of Monivaird and Strowan was not held, "in regarde of the great tempest and storme of weather quhilk fell out upon the day appointed" and a new visit was ordained for the last Tuesday of October 1666, to consider the convenience of one kirk for the two paroches, and of a sufficient passage, together with the establishing of a reader and school. (By passage is, no doubt, meant a crossing over or through the Earn by a ford).

"April 10th. 1667. Mr John Phillipe, expectant, recommended to preach four tymes at Comrie, now for the present being vacant." (Mr Phillipe's name given also as Philp or Philip). In 1667, the Rev. Mr Row, Minister of the joint parishes of Monzievaird and Strowan was successful in getting a new church built at Enoch for the accommodation of the united parishes. This church never built, so ordained that the kirk of Strowan be the only parish kirk. On 21st. July 1669, Mr Row produced to the Presbytery "ane Act of Synod to cause the Lairds of Monzievaird, Ochtertyre, Fordie, Clathick, Aberlednock and others, to come to the kirk of Strowan, as now the onlie parish kirk."

Admonitions and directions were given to the clergy as to the exercise of discipline. "Not only scandals of unchastity, but drunkenness, swearing, cursing, filthy speaking, so usual among the common sort in their house or field labour, mocking of religion, and all other offences", were to be enquired into and censured.

"Against common and crying sins, such as swearing, cursing, railing, rotten and filthy speaking so usual among the common sort in their house and field labour, together, particulerlie in harvest and that all ministers recommend to the owners of cropes and overseers of the reapers to range them so to their work and such divisions as may give least occasione for anything of that kinde."

"April 24th. 1668. For preventing of tippling and drinking in aill houses upon the Lord's Day, it is ordained that the bell of the paroch church be runge about halfe ane houre after afternoones sermone and if that they sal be found in aill houses after the said bell, then those persones are to be censured by the minister and session; lykewise, hyreing of servantes on the Lord's Day to be curbed."

"April 25th. 1668. To endeavour and use all meanes possible to cause the people within their severall congregatiounes at weddings and feastes to absteine from intemperance and profane jesting, and the too great libertie they take of undecent behaviour in their promiscuous danceings."

"April 25th. 1668. Agreid that the contribucioun for the harbour of Kilburne be collected thorowout the wholl churches of the Diocese."

There being no Poor Law in Scotland, no Insurance companies, no Public Works Commissions, great part of what is now the work of Government and other National bodies, fell directly on the people themselves. A Certificate of Communicant Membership in a kirk not only permitted the holder to partake of the Holy Sacrament, it acted as a sort of local passport. Each parish was responsible for its own poor, for example, and there are many cases of vagrants being returned to their parish of origin. But charity often extended far beyond the parish and no deserving stranger, if destitute, would be passed on his way unaided. The Sabbath Plate Collections went directly into the Poors' Box, and was dispensed at the discretion of the Minister and Session at regular intervals. Special collections were taken at kirk doors for such subjects as building or repairing bridges and harbours, the rebuilding of homes burned down, supply of goods and gear if lost by fire or at sea. Intimations of country-wide collections would be passed down from the Privy Council to the General Assembly of the Kirk, to Presbyteries and Kirk Sessions. Local need and charity was supplied by local initiative. We read of many such cases, both within the parish and further afield as we read through these Session and Presbyterial Registers of long ago.

"October 13th. 1668. The Bishop and Synod referres the bussines anent the new erection of the kirk of Monivaird and Strowane to the Presbytery of Ochterardor."

"Aprill 14th. 1669. The Synod haveing information that the busines of setting of one kirk for the parochines of Strowane and Monivaird has been pursued and one kirk, to witt, the kirk of Strowane ordained to be the place for publiq worshipe in all tyme to come; and takeing notice that some heritores and severall boundes within the said paroch doe not repaire to publiq worshipe at the paroch kirk ordained by publiq authority; doe therefore by thir presents require such heritores both to repair thereto themselves and cause the people within their boundes to doe the lyk, otherwyse the Synod cannot neglectt such unorderlie cariage, so stronglie savoureing of neglectt, not only of the ordinances, but also of the civill authority; have ordained the Presbyterie to make their redresse to his Majestie's counsell for reparacioun thereoff."

Minute of Presbytery. "Comrie, June 3rd. 1669—The quhilk day being appoynted for visiting the Kirk of Comrie, Mr Jas. Rowe of Strowand preached from Titus ii, 7. Mr John Philp, Minister of the church, was inquirit if he made public intimation of the visitation from the pulpit, according as he was enjoined, to which, affirmative. Whereupon the Moderator and brethren present proceeded and first of all did require ane list of his elders' names, who were named by him:- Jas. Drummond of Comrie; Patrick Comrie of Ross; Thos.

Drummond of Dalchonzie; Donald McNiven of Dalich-lanie (probably Dalclathick); Alex. McNiven of Maler; Duncan Robertson in Dalginross; Duncan Morrison in Glenlednock; Wm. Drummond in Dundurne; Malcolm Stalker in Great Moret; and Patrick McGregor in Earnlie. The elders being callit, compeared Jas. Drummond of Comrie; Patrick Comrie, Alex McNiven and Wm. Drummond. The foresaid gentilmen heritors were called in and judiciously sworn by holding up their hands to declair and answer those quiries that were to be proposed to them, in order as to the minister's life and doctrine.

1stlie. Jas. Drummond was posed if the minister preached sound and edifying doctrine? Answerit affirmative.

2ndlie. If he was blameless in his life? Answerit affirmative.

3rdlie. If he preached twyce everie Lord's Day? Answerit affirmative.

4thlie. If he catechised everie week except seedtime and harvest? Answerit affirmative.

5thlie. If he celebrate the sacrament? Answerit affirmative.

6thlie. If he pressed family worship? Answerit affirmative.

7thlie. Whether the Holy Scriptures were publicly read everie Lord's Day, and some portions read after the minister is in the pulpit? Answerit affirmative.

8thlie. If the doxologie was used? Answerit affirmative.

9thlie. If he visited the sick? Answerit for aught he knew, he did it.

10thlie. Whether he had cups, basins, and laver for celebration of the Sacrament? Answerit negative.

And further being inquired if he pressed a reverent gesture in prayer? Answerit: that he did it sometimes.

The minister being than askit anent his grievances if he had ane manse. Answerit affirmative. Being inquirit anent the provision of the Kirk? Answerit:

that he had 64 merks or thereabout. Being askit about the situation of the kirk? Answerit that it was in the east end of the parish.

If he had provision for a schoolmaster? Answer, there was once ane, but not now. He regraits the want of glass windows, and a bridge, and the want of a churchyaird dyk.

April 14th. 1674. The said day it being reported to the Synod that in a hostile manner some persones did raise a dead corp after that it was buried, and did interre it in another place in the kirkycard of Strowane, their determinacioun is, that both the persones who buried within ryt of other men, and these who raised the corp, be cited unto and censured by the session of the said parish for publiq achknowledgement of such ane enormouse transgression, and recommend it to the shireff or deputes of the shyre to be assisted.

April 9th. 1678. Recommended to the ministers to be careful to collect for the prisoners under the Turks' slavery."

"April 10th. 1678. The Bishop and Synod taking to their consideration that some pairts of the parish of Comrie lies far distant from the parish kirk, and nearer to the kirk of Balquhidder; lykewise some pairts of the united parish of Strowand and Monivaird lies far distant from the said kirks, and nearer to Comrie,--did therefore find it most convenient that the people dwelling in these pairts doe resort to those respective kirks which are nearest to them for all Church benefits and censures; whereunto all the three ministers of the kirks aforesaid have agreed, and given their assent in tyme to come according to the conditions of the Synod."

Mr Philip is still the minister at the Presbytery Visit of 1679--"the said Johne being asked if his elders were blameless, declared that they were the best he could have." *(What precisely this answer meant, we have now no way of knowing).*

On the 24th. November 1682, a letter was received

19

from the Bishop "desiring the Moderator to put the brethren in mind of what the law requires of them concerning disorderly persons in their bounds; and that to the Lords of His Majestie's Council an account must be given of their names this month, and that those who are short of their duty will come to greater trouble than they are aware of." The ministers were accordingly required to give in the names of disorderly persons within their respective parishes, when Mr John Philp, Comrie, "declared under his hand that he knew none; which declaration, of his being, as he says, a matter of verity, he trusts it will be accepted."

It was during the time of Bishop Ramsay that the sad affair of the minister of Kinkell occurred. Richard Duncan, M.A., graduated in Edinburgh in 1667; was licensed by the Bishop of Edinburgh in 1673. On the 1st. July 1674, "a letter was delivered to the Moderator in judicio by Mr Richard Duncan, expectant, in order to the entering of him for trials to the kirk of Kinkell."

He was taken on trial accordingly, and ordained and admitted prior to 11th. November 1674; he was in good repute for some years, but came to a sad and untimely end. On the 13th. July 1681 he was libelled by the Laird of Machanie and others for immoral conduct, and gross and scandalous misdemeanours, and deposed before the 1st. of February following. Afterwards, the remains of a child having been found in the Manse, buried under the hearthstone, he was tried as an accessory to murder, condemned to death by the Steward of Strathearn, and executed at Crieff the same year. A reprieve having been ordained in his favour, the bearer of it was seen approaching on horseback at full speed by way of Muthill, but the work of execution was hurried, and the messenger arrived a few minutes too late. *(Muthill disputes with Crieff the "honour" of the execution).*

(This is probably the actuality behind the old verse:

"O what a parish, sic a terrible parish,
O what a parish is that of Kinkell!

They hae hangit the minister, drooned the precentor,
Dang doon the Steeple, and drucken the bell."

It is the tradition that the precentor was drowned in fording the Earn at Kinkell. The kirk bell was sold and is now said to be in Cockpen.)

"April 25th. 1682. Presented to the Bishop and Synod ane Act of His Majestie's Privy Council in favoures of the burgh of Dunbarton, granting warrand for a voluntarie contribution to be collected throughout the whole kingdom towards the building of ane stone bridge upon the River Leven, recommending to the Archbishops and Bishops to cause the ministers in their respective Dioceses to make intimation of the said voluntarie contribution, and to see the same charitablie performed."

"April 10th. 1683. Bishop recommended to the brethren the Act of Council for a voluntarie contribution towards the building and repairing the harbour of Aberdeene."

In October 1684, Robert Douglas was appointed Bishop of Dunblane. "Bishop recommends to brethren the Act of Council in favours of the afflicted inhabitants of the town of Kelso through the late fire, for a voluntarie contribution."

April 13th. 1686. Contribution for the distressed people of Newburgh, who has sustained great loss through fire.

April 12th. 1687. Mr Philp, minister at Comrie, being verie often absent from Synod is recommended by the Bishop to observe the dyets of the Presbyterie better in tyme coming.

April 12th. 1687. Voluntarie contribution asked for repairing the bridge of Newmilnes.

Mr John Philp, minister of Comrie, was deprived on the 17th. September 1689 for not reading the Proclamation and refusing to pray for their Majesties William and Mary; but, like many other ejected ministers in Jacobite districts, he continued to officiate in the parish for many years after the re-establishment of

B

presbytery.

In April 1693, the Synod drew up "ane account of the grievances within the province", in which complaint is made that "there be among us many of the Prelatical persuasion, who have been deprived by their Majesties' Privy Countil, or deposed by Church judicatories for gross scaldals; who, notwithstanding, do intrude themselves upon vacant churches", etc. Then follows a list of the names of the ministers who had been guilty of such irregularities among whom is specified Mr John Philp, in the parish of Comrie.

Ruins of pre-reformation Chapel of Dundurn, burial place of the Stewarts of Ardvorlich.

Tullichettle Kirkyard showing outline of ancient chapel and the memorial table stone of the McGrouthers of Meigar.

CHAPTER IV

POST REFORMATION MINISTERS

TULLICHETIL

1572. **John Edmeston,** exhorter at Lammas, 1572.
1574. **William Drummond,** eldest son of David Drummond of Mylnab, minister of Crieff, in 1574 had charge of Comrie, Monzievaird, Monzie and Tullichetil; translated to Strageath about 1576.

COMRIE AND TULLICHETIL

These parishes were united in the 16th. century. DUNDURN was also joined with them, but it was severed in 1894, to be linked again with the joint parishes of COMRIE and STROWAN in 1979.

The church of COMRIE was dedicated to St. Kessog. It belonged to the Abbey of Paisley. A fair of St. Kessog was held here on the 10th. of March. It seems probable that TULLICHETIL is the post-Reformation name of the parish of TULLIEDENE whose church of St. Serf was bestowed on the Austin Canons of the Abbey of Inchaffray by Gilbert, Earl of Strathearn, early in the 13th. century. (Charters of Inchaffray Abbey).

1567. **Duncan Comrie** was reader in 1567. He died in 1574.
1576. **Malcolm Comrie** was reader in 1576 to 1580.

c

1585. **Alexander Chisholm,** removed from Muthill, with that parish, STROWAN and TULLICHETIL also in his charge in 1585; translated to LECROPT in 1588.

1588. **John Davidson, M.A.,** minister of COMRIE in 1588, with MUTHILL and others in his charge, removed to MUTHILL before August 1590. He was one of the 42 ministers who signed the Protest to Parliament against the introduction of Episcopacy. 1st. July 1606 he was named constant Moderator in 1606 and died April 1607, aged about 45.

1598. **John Monteath, M.A.,** presented by James VI, 26th. June 1598, translated to BALQUHIDDER about 1599, but returned in 1602; translated to AUCHTERARDER in 1603.

1608. **George Callum** (or McCallum or McGillichallum), presented by James VI, 23rd. February 1608, having BALQUHIDDER, STROWAN, TULLI-CHETIL, and MONZIEVAIRD also in his charge; removed to BALQUHIDDER before 1614.

1618. **Andrew Young,** son of Andrew Young of Dunblane, admitted before 1618; died in 1619.

1629. **Archibald McLaughlan,** minister in 1629.

THE TIME OF THE BISHOPS

The following three ministers were in office during the Time of the Bishops.

1635. **James Graham, M.A.,** admitted about 1635; suspended in 1649 for having subscribed "the divisive supplication and unlawful engagement"; on professing sorrow for his offence, he was reponed in 1650. At meeting of Synod in 1641 he is "markit non-resident". The Presbytery was ordered to make all ministers "to dwell within their awin parochines before the 29th.

September or then deprive them." Translated
to Glendevon in 1655.

1656. "Mr. John Murray of Coldon (Cowden) and Patrick
Comrie of Ross, Commissioners from the Paroch
of Comrie appeared and earnestly desired that
the said Mr. Hugh Gordon might be transported
from Fortingall to Comrie with all convenience
in regard to their desolate condition." **Hugh
Gordon** translated from Fortingall to Comrie
between 9th. April and 14th. October 1656;
translated to Row (Rhu) in 1665.

1668. **John Philip,** son of Duncan Philip of Coldoun;
educated at St. Andrews University, M.A., 1663;
admitted before 29th. April 1668; deposed 17th.
September 1689 for not obeying the Proclamation
of the Estates, and not praying for William
and Mary, but continued for some time, and
mentioned by the Synod as guilty of irregularities
12th. April 1693.

1692. **John McKercher, M.A.,** called 31st. March 1692;
ordained 15th. March 1693; translated to DULL,
7th. June 1699.

1701. **John McCallum,** called 16th. December 1701;
ordained 31st. March 1702; translated to CAL-
LANDER, 10th. November 1709.

1710. **Dugald Campbell,** called 28th. June 1710; ordained
4th. May 1711; translated to LISMORE and
APPIN, 28th. October 1719. During his time
in 1711, at a Presbytery Visitation, estimates
were taken for a minister's manse, 46 feet in
length over walls and 10 feet in breadth, with
office, houses and yard-dykes thereunto belonging.
Tradesmen to be John Ross, mason, Will Comrie,
wright, and two honest men, indwellers in Comrie,
Duncan Galloch and John Miller.

1721. **Patrick McAdam, M.A.,** called 16th. March
and ordained 11th. May 1721; died, unmarried,
March 1722, aged about 28.

1723. **Andrew Muschet,** or **Mushet** was called August

and ordained 26th. September 1723, "having been recommended by an elder who had heard from the Balquhidder minister that he had 'preached well in the Irish in his kirk'."

In February 1728, Mr. Muschet wrote to Colin Campbell of Aberuchill, one of the heritors, that "the bridge of Comrie being in such a tottering state etc., I was obliged to send an express to Sir James (Campbell) and Monzie that part of the vacant stipend be assessed for that use."

In June 1725, Mr. Muschet petitioned for a bridge, probably that at Dalclathick, on the grounds that "one of the Charity Schools in the parish is like to be rendered inaccessible by a stream interjecting between it and the district of the parish from which most of the scholars used to come." (It seems likely that this school was the Glenartney one, opened in the early 18th. century by the S.S.P.C.K. There were eventually five such in the parish.)

In July 1728, Mr. Muschet described the Sacrament:- "The Lord had favoured us with fair seasonable weather. We had near eleven tables in Irish. Each table contained 48 persons or thereabout and we had only two tables and some few persons at the 3rd. in English. The people as to outward appearance behave extraordinarily well so that there was no disturbance or disorder notwithstanding of the languages. I had the assistance of 10 ministers from the beginning to the end of the week."

(Perhaps these figures of over 500 in Gaelic and about 100 in English are a true reflection of the language position in Upper Strathearn in the early years of the 18th. century).

Mr. Muschet died in 1731.

1731. **Aeneas Shaw,** called 19th. August and ordained December 1731; translated to PETTY on 8th. June 1742.

1743. **Robert Menzies, M.A.,** missionary at Glenalmond, called 30th March and ordained 7th. September 1743. He died at Stirling in 1780, aged about 74. It was Mr. Menzies who in 1745 rode all the way to Carlisle to intercede with the Duke of Cumberland for some of the parishioners who had taken part in the Pretender's army under the Earl of Perth in the '45 Rising.

1781. **Hugh McDiarmid,** ordained to the Gaelic Chapel of Ease, Glasgow, was presented to COMRIE by George III on 29th. January and admitted 13th. July 1781. He died 4th. November 1801. Mr. McDiarmid wrote many lengthy poems in Gaelic and made a study of the Roman Camp of Dalginross. He believed that the Battle of Mons Graupius was fought in Upper Strathearn and left a highly fanciful account of the battle which he thought had ranged from the side of Loch Earn to around Monzievaird and up into the hills about Innergeldie. His definitions of some Gaelic place-names in this district do not find confirmation with some modern Gaelic place-name scholars. He was due to write the First Statistical Account of Comrie in 1795, but owing to his ill-health, this was undertaken by the minister of Monzievaird, the Rev. Mr. Colin Baxter. Dogged by illness, Mr. McDiarmid had an ordained assistant, the Rev. John McLaren.

1802. **Patrick McIsaac,** born 1774; minister at GASK in 1798; presented by George III 20th. March and admitted 12th. August 1802. He died January 1829.

1829. **William McKenzie,** from Inverness, presented by George IV, 4th. April and ordained 23rd. July 1829; translated to DUNBLANE, 1841, and to North Leith Free Church in 1844.

1841. **James Carment,** born Glasgow in March 1816, son of David Carment, minister of ROSKEEN;

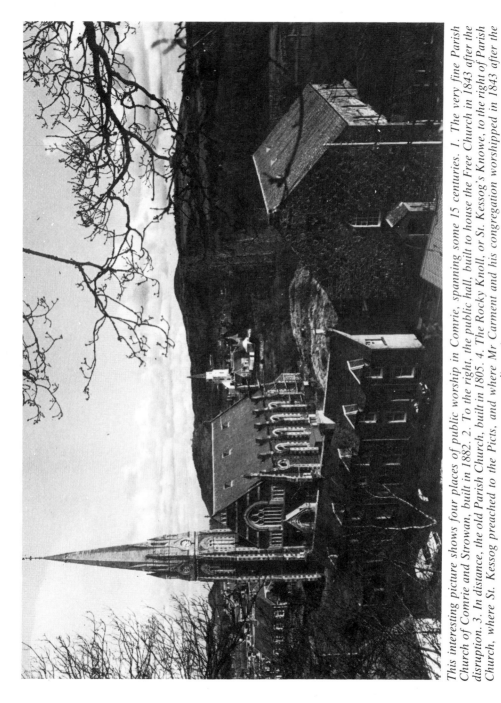

This interesting picture shows four places of public worship in Comrie, spanning some 15 centuries. 1. The very fine Parish Church of Comrie and Strowan, built in 1882. 2. To the right, the public hall, built to house the Free Church in 1843 after the disruption. 3. In distance, the old Parish Church, built in 1805. 4. The Rocky Knoll, or St. Kessog's Knowe, to the right of Parish Church, where St. Kessog preached to the Picts, and where Mr Carment and his congregation worshipped in 1843 after the disruption.

presented by Queen Victoria, 13th. May 1841. Joined the Free Church at the Disruption of 1843 and was minister of the Free Church, COMRIE until his death on 19th. January 1880.

1843. **John McDonald,** born 1794 at Kinloch Rannoch, son of Duncan McDonald, farmer and Ann Stewart. Translated from Kenmore and admitted 26th. September 1843. D.D. Glasgow 1855. He died, unmarried in 1875.

(In 1842 the stipend was £250. 9. 1, with two glebes, one for Comrie and one for Tullichetil of £15. 10s., one of the best in Scotland.)

1875. **John MacPherson,** born at Kilmelford, in 1837; ordained to Gaelic Church, GREENOCK in 1865; translated and admitted to COMRIE on 5th. August 1875. He died 2nd. July 1911.

1911. **Andrew Blair Wann,** born at Perth, 1862; assistant St. Michael's, Edinburgh; ordained missionary to Bombay; Principal of Scottish Churches College, Calcutta, 1908-1909; D.D. 1909; admitted to Comrie, September 1911. He died 28th. June 1923.

1924. **Charles William Parish, M.C., B.D.,** translated from Bothkennar, December 1924; translated to MUIRTON-MARYKIRK (Arbuthnott) 1933.

1929. FORMATION OF THE CHURCH OF SCOTLAND

(The former Parish Church became "COMRIE OLD" and Comrie U.F. Church became "COMRIE ST. KESSOG'S").

COMRIE OLD

Charles William Parish. (See above).

1934. **Archibald MacBride Hunter, B.D., Ph.D.,** ordained and inducted 29th. March 1934; demitted on appointment as Yates Professor of New Testament Greek, Mansfield College, Oxford in 1937, and later as Professor of New Testament Studies in Aberdeen.

1937. **George Wilson Hamilton, B.D.,** translated from Knightswood, St. Margaret's, December 1937; demitted October 1948 and died September 1950.

1949. **Patrick Douglas Gordon Campbell, M.A.,** ordained and inducted April 1949; demitted 1956 and translated to Tillicultry; St. Serf's, October 1956.

THE PRESBYTERIAN CHURCH IN SCOTLAND

To explain the multiplicity of kirk buildings in Comrie, it will be helpful to state some of the permutations and combinations of congregations which have taken place here.

Under William and Mary in 1690, Presbyterianism was established as the state church in Scotland. The independent rights of the church were safeguarded in the Act of Union of 1707. Under Queen Anne in 1712 an important act, in the future to be the cause of great trouble and strife, allowed "patrons", usually the Crown or great landlords, to present appointments of ministers, even on hostile parishioners.

In 1733, Ebenezer Erskine of Stirling, a powerful preacher, denounced all limitation of the power of the congregation to choose its own minister. Deposed with several associates by the General Assembly in 1740, they founded the first Scottish free church, later known as the Secession Church. Further divisions within the Secession Church occurred, but the breaches were healed in 1820 and the church now took the name of the United Secession Church.

The question of patronage was still a running sore and a further break took place in 1761 when several ministers founded what became the Relief Church.

That these feelings ran strongly among the people is shown by the fact that some 100,000 persons in 1765 adhered to the various Secession kirks. In 1847, the United Secession Church and the Relief Church combined as the United Presbyterian Church.

In 1843, after years of un-Christian dispute and anger, took place within the Established Church, the most momentous event since the Reformation—the Disruption. Some four hundred and seventy-four ministers, under the leadership of Thomas Chalmers, walked out of the General Assembly of the state church and formed the Free Church of Scotland. They gave up parishes and salaries. All had to start afresh.

Later, in 1874, the rights of patronage, the original ground of division, were abolished by law, and in 1900, the vast majority of the Free Church of Scotland and the United Presbyterian Church joined in one body as the United Free Church of Scotland. Finally In 1929 the union took place of the United Free Church and the Established Church with the name, Church of Scotland.

FREE CHURCH

As shown in 1841, the Rev. James Carment was presented to Comrie as the minister of the Established Church, the Parish Kirk. In 1843 he was one of the ministers who "came out", taking most of his parishioners with him. Like his brothers in like case, he gave up church, manse and stipend. All had to be begun anew. For a time, the congregation worshipped in the open on the rocky knoll to the west of the present church—St.Kessog's Knowe. Within a year his folk had provided a church, now the Public Hall, and a school in Dundas Street. After being housed in Dalginross for a short period, Mr. Carment took up residence in a new manse, now Oakleigh in The Ross. In 1879 the foundations of the new church were laid, through the magnificent legacy of £9 000 from Miss MARY MACFARLANE. Sadly, Mr. Carment died in 29th. January 1880 before the building was completed.

THE FREE CHURCH

1880. **Charles Kay,** inducted 8th. June 1880.
1888. **Arthur Crawford Watt, M.A.,** ordained 19th. January 1888; translated to Crailing in 1924 to allow of the union of the West and East churches under the name of Comrie United Free Church, with one minister. Mr. Watt died 17th. March 1934. (The west church became the place of workship of the united congregation and the former east church was later bought by the Parish Church and was named the Dr. Wann Memorial Hall).
1925. **Allan M'Donald Craig, M.A.,** inducted 1925; translated to Castleton 1931. Retired October 1960 and died 3rd. July 1963.

THE CHURCH OF SCOTLAND

1929. Formation of the Church of Scotland by the union of the Parish Church and the United Free Church. In Comrie, the west church took the name of Comrie St. Kessog's, while the parish Church was named Comrie Old.

ST. KESSOG'S

1930. **Ian Darroch Neilson, M.A.,** translated from Cambusnethan North, February 1922, demitted March 1948, and died 11 April 1966.
1948. **George Brown Cameron Sangster, D.S.C., B.D.,**

ordained and inducted October 1948, translated to Aberdeen Queen's Cross, October 1953.

1954. **Daniel Moncrieff M'Aulay,** introduced August 1954; died 5th. June 1956.

1956. **Iverach McDonald,** locum tenens October 1956.

1956. December 9th. Comrie Old and St. Kessog's congregations united under the name of Comrie Old and St. Kessog's. (St. Kessog's Church building became the place of worship and Comrie Old building became Comrie Youth and Community Centre).

COMRIE OLD AND ST. KESSOG'S

1957. **William Paton Henderson, B.D., B.Ed.,** translated from Gullane and inducted 9th. July 1957; demitted to take up lectureship in Religious Education, Aberdeen College of Education, 30th. September 1961; returned to parish ministry and inducted to linked charge of Fortingall and Glenlyon, 27th. January 1966.

1962. **John M'Ghie,** translated from Aberdeen Greyfriars and inducted 21st. March 1962.

1964. Comrie Old and St. Kessog's united with Monzievaird and Strowan (West Section) under the name of Comrie and Strowan, September 1964.

COMRIE AND STROWAN

1964. **John M'Ghie,** became minister of united charge, 2nd. September 1964; retired 28 February 1967.

1967. **Robert James Stewart, B.D., S.T.M.,** inducted 5th. July 1967, translated from Wishaw St. Mary's. Translated to Bothwell, 1978.

1978. **Peter Thomson, M.A., B.D.,** inducted 27th. April 1978.

1979. Comrie and Strowan linked with Dundurn, St. Fillans.

Old Kirk and Kirkyard of Strowan. Fine memorial inscription and armorial bearings of John Murray of Strowan, ancestor of the Dukes of Atholl.

The author and Bill Gardiner at the Market Cross of Strowan.

THE PRESBYTERIAN CHURCH IN SCOTLAND

1733. The Original Secession.

1740. The United Societies of Strathearn were formed. The persons assembling in Comrie met generally in the open air on the north bank of the Earn, just west of the junction with the Lednock, until 1752, when a church was erected on ground leased for 2000 years. This church was replaced in 1794 by one seating 500 with an adjoining manse. This was in Samuel Gilfillan's time and, in its derelict state, is still known as "The Gilfillan Kirk". It is the ruinous building, with rusty corrugated iron roof seen by one looking N.E. from Dalginross Bridge.

    A new church was built in what was known as Renwick Street in 1866. The cost was £1500 and it had seatings for 350 persons. It was built in the time of the Rev. William Swan. It was, of course, the United Presbyterian Church which had been formed previously in 1847.

1746. **John Muckersie,** ordained in 1746 and had charge of Kinkell, Comrie and Muthill.

1758. **John Ferguson,** ordained 1758 and died 1760. He was also minister of Greenloaning.

1775. In 1775, Comrie petitioned for sermon in Gaelic and Mr. Laing was sent to them for some time. In the same year, Comrie and Crieff were disjoined and Comrie became vacant.

1791. **Samuel Gilfillan,** ordained April 1791. He died 15th. October 1826, aged 64 years. He was the father of the great George Gilfillan of Dundee, immensely popular as a preacher in his day.

    Samuel Gilfillan's salary never exceeded £90 a year. There is a record of his income and expenditures for the year ended 30th. December 1803 which shows;

```
-- Total income to be    £62.  14s.   0.
   Total expenditure     £61.   6s.  10.
        Left over         £1.   7s.   2.
```

Thanks to God for all His Mercies, Spiritual and Temporal, His Blessings maketh rich.

1830. **James Mitchell,** ordained September 1830. He died on 2nd. January 1835 in his 34th. year, "his constitution said to have been weakened by tea and tobacco".

1837. **Robert Thomson Walker,** ordained January 1837. He was accused of holding opinions of James Morrison, who afterwards founded a new denomination. His case was several times before the Synod and Presbytery, but no further action was taken. Translated to Dunfermline in 1844. He thereafter removed to Australia, and in 1874 he occupied the position of Moderator of the Assembly of Victoria.

1848. **William Swan,** ordained June 1848. Retired through ill-health, June 1881.

1882. **William Hall,** ordained 1882. With the formation of the United Free Church in 1900, the U.P. church was named the East United Free Church. Mr. Hall retired in 1924 when the two U.F. Church congregations joined to form one congregation in the West Church.

DUNDURN

The ancient parish of DUNDURN was united to Comrie and Tullichetil in the 16th. century. The minister of Comrie was required to hold one service each month. It was severed from Comrie on 15th. March 1895 under its own minister, but linked again with Comrie and Strowan Church in 1979.

The original church was dedicated to St. Fillan of Rathearn, known variously as the Leper or Stammerer. At Dunfillan, within the parish, are St. Fillan's Well and St. Fillan's Chair.

In 1879, Peter Drummond of Drumearn, Comrie, an ardent Free Churchman, erected a small church at St. Fillans for the Free Church adherents. This church was served by the Free/United Free Church minister of Comrie who took an afternoon service there on the first and third Sunday, each month. That arrangement ceased in 1929 when the former St. Fillans U.F. congregation was united with the former Church of Scotland. The building was subsequently acquired by the Episcopal Church.

1895. **Thomas Armstrong,** born 1855, ordained to St. Fillan's Chapel, September 1881. Admitted first minister of the parish April 1895. He died in September 1907.

(There would appear at this date 1895, to have been a missionary Hall at Glentarken, as there exists a record of Mr. Joseph Dick, Comrie doing some plumber work in the hall).

1908. **Adam Wylie Hempseed Scott,** ordained 1908.

1930. **David John McLaren, M.A.,** translated from Trinity Gask, May 1930; demitted July 1951 and died 6 March 1960.

1952. **Robert Alexander Robertson, M.A.,** translated from Dundee Maryfield, and inducted February 1952. Demitted 1957 and translated to Edinburgh Nicholson Street, 12 June 1957.

1958. **William Paterson, B.Sc.,** translated from Newport St. Fillans and inducted February 1958; retired January 1967.

1967. **Anderson Nicol, D.D.,** translated from Aberdeen West & St. Nicholas and inducted June 1967; died 1st. August 1972.

1973. **John H.G. Ross,** translated from Edinburgh Fairmilehead and inducted March 1973; retired 1979.

Church linked with Comrie and Strowan Church in 1979.

Post Reformation Ministers

MONZIEVAIRD

The church here was dedicated to St. Serf. It belonged to the Abbey of Inchaffray. Beside the church was St. Serf's Well.

1564. **Alexander Christison,** probably Christie, the last Roman Vicar of Crieff, was reader from 1564 to 1567.
1569. **Thomas Glas,** reader from 1569 to 1574, in which year he died.
1572. **William Drummond,** minister of Crieff, in charge 1572.
1576. **John Malloch,** reader, 1576 to 1577.
1580. **Andrew Malloch,** reader, 1580 to 1590.

STROWAN or STRUAN

Called often Strowan Stirling. The church was dedicated to St. Ronan. Close to it was St. Ronan's Well and very near the church, too, is Pol Ronain, Ronan's Pool in the Earn. A fair here was called Feill Ronain.

1564. **James Murray,** reader from 1564 to 1567.
1572. **Alexander Gail,** minister at Muthill, in charge in 1572.
1585. **Alexander Chisholm,** minister of Comrie, removed from Muthill, with that parish, Strowan and Tullichetil in his charge in 1585. Translated to Lecropt in 1588.
1586. **Norman Leslie,** parson from 1586 to 1590.

The two parishes of Monzievaird and Strowan were united about the end of the 16th. century.

MONZIEVAIRD AND STROWAN

1608. **George Callum,** minister of Comrie, in charge around 1608.

1623. **Henry Anderson, M.A.,** born 1589, admitted about 1623, died June 1641. He married Marion (died between 1650 and 1660) daughter of James Redheuch of Aberlednock.

1642. **George Murray, M.A.,** admitted in 1642; translated to Foulis Wester between November 1645 and April 1646.

1648. **William Wemyss, M.A.,** admitted before April 1648. Translated to Dron, 1653.

1655. **James Row, M.A.,** admitted to Muthill in 1635, deposed February 1645 for favouring the Royal cause, but was reponed on recommendation of the Synod by the Assembly, October 1650, and admitted here in 1655. Had a grant of £50 from Parliament, July 1661, on account of his sufferings. Still minister 21st. January 1680. He married Margaret, daughter of William Stirling of Ardoch.

1680. **George Mitchell, M.A.,** ordained and admitted April 1680. He married Catherine Toseach.

1680. **George Young, M.A.,** admitted (at Strowan) September 1680. Deposed by the Privy Council, September 1689 for not reading the Proclamation of the Estates, nor praying for William and Mary, but for James VII. He was alive in 1694.

1692. **John Campbell,** admitted (at Strowan) June 1692. He died March 1721.

1721. **William Duncan,** born 1682, ordained August 1721 and died March 1729.

1730. **James Porteous, M.A.,** of Dalvich, born 1701. Ordained August 1730 and died 1780.

1776. **William Thomson,** born 1746, ordained assistant March 1776 but demitted October 1778. Devoted himself thereafter to literary pursuits in London. Ll.D., Glasgow 1783. He died March 1817.

1781. **Colin Baxter,** presented by Thomas Robert, Earl of Kinnoull, April and ordained August 1781. He wrote accounts of the parishes of Monzievaird and Strowan and of Comrie for the Old Statistical Account of Scotland.

1843. **William Robertson,** born 1830, ordained September 1843; died June 1864. He wrote the hymns "A little child, the Saviour came" and "Thee God we praise, Thee Lord Confess".

1864. **John Robert Campbell,** born 1834, translated from Ardoch and admitted November 1864; died 1894.

1895. **The Hon. Arthur Gordon, M.A.,** born 1854, translated and admitted May 1895. He resigned in 1902.

1903. **David Heggie, M.A.,** born 1874, ordained May 1903. Joined Army and was Chaplain to Royal Scots during First World War. Died Curragh Camp, October 1917.

1918. **William Wilson Bell,** translated and admitted May 1918. Removed to Craigneuk October 1928.

1929. **Alexander Bain Harper,** born 1886, admitted September 1929; demitted September 1951 and died November 1952.

1952. **William Baildon Taylor,** inducted September 1952; retired September 1964. He died 22nd. August 1969.

1965. Monzievaird and Strowan Church closed 1965. The building was later demolished. The western portion of the congregation joined with Comrie to form Comrie and Strowan Church, while the eastern portion joined with Crieff South to form Crieff South and Monzievaird Church.

CHAPTER V

ROADS AND BRIDGES

The building of roads and bridges and their adequate maintenance are essential to civilisation. Without them there can be no regular communication between persons and places and no government can hope to exercise control where they do not exist. This was a lesson which the Roman conquerors of South Britain well knew and took strenuous steps to achieve. However, unlike in the south, in Scotland, Rome's efforts were mere pinpricks of punitive expeditions, and no great steps appear to have been taken by her to set up a lasting network of roads connecting our local camps with those to the south and east. It is altogether likely that they merely made use of the existing tracks of the inhabitants, largely confined to the higher ground, well above the levels of rivers and marshes.

Such roads as they may have made were created for military purposes and fell into disrepair after their departure as they were of little use to the native inhabitants. And so, in much of Scotland, and in the Highlands in particular, little or no effort was put into building of roads or bridges until the early 18th. century when Government set General Wade to building a system of roads for military purposes to facilitate the rapid movement of troops between the forts and barracks of the north, after the 1715 Rebellion.

Of course, there were roads of a sort before Wade's time. Is there not a rhyme?

Roads and Bridges

"If you had seen these roads
before they were made,
You would lift up your hands,
and bless General Wade."

To describe such tracks as there were, as roads, would be an abuse of terms. If we are to believe the statements of all travellers in the Highlands well into the 18th. century, we must assume that any travel was of the nature of an expedition into uncharted country. In wet summers roads would become quagmires, and in winter, often quite impassable. There being few or no bridges, the passing of rivers by fords or ferries was hazardous in the extreme. One went on foot or horseback. Wheeled traffic was unknown and was scarcely possible before the early years of the 19th. century. Even then, we have tales of carriages being upset, of wheels breaking and axles snapping.

In 1724 Major-General George Wade was sent to Scotland "narrowly to inspect the present situation of the Highlanders ...and to suggest such other remedies as may conduce to the good settlement of that part of the Kingdom".

The concluding part of his report is of significance: "The Highlands are still more impracticable, from the want of roads and bridges". There are no military roads as such within the bounds of our parish but several pass within short distances. Not all were built at the direction of Wade. Indeed, during Wade's time in Scotland until his departure in 1740, and under General Clayton till he was succeeded by Johnnie Cope in 1743, the task of inspection and construction of the roads fell to Major William Caulfeild until he, too, was succeeded by Colonel Skene.

During the years 1725 to 1737 some 250 miles of Military Roads were built in the Highlands, including that from Dalnacardoch by Tummel Bridge to Crieff. In 1741 and 1742 a military road from Stirling to Crieff was constructed, while from 1749 a road was built from Stirling to Fort William by Callander, Lochearnhead and through Glen Ogle by Lochan Lairig Ilidh to Crianlarich. Only in parts, in their decayed state, can these particular roads be traced, as modern roadbuilders often followed the old lines. A few bridges still in use can be attributed to the military builders, that at Aberfeldy being a masterpiece of Wade's. It is no more correct to call a bridge a Wade bridge than to call any a Roman Bridge, of which there are none in Scotland. One may speak of a Wade-style bridge, but only in so far as the bridge is an aged, arched structure in local stone, built usually, by the master masons of each district. Wade and his soldier engineers need not have come within a hundred miles of them.

Of course there were made roads, other than mere tracks traced out by the hooves of garrons and feet of folk, long before the time of Wade. We have few early maps to show us how these ran, but from the positions of the various clachans and farmtouns in our area, we can assume that movement between them had to take place, and these early routes can be traced today on the ground. Their position and line are confirmed by the earliest maps we have. Folks had to get to kirk and market in order to satisfy their spiritual needs and obligations, as also to obtain some necessities of life by purchase or exchange.

During the early part of the 17th. century, the additional duty was laid on the Justices of the Peace to overlook and see to the repair of roads to churches and market places, but their powers were so limited that little or nothing was done to implement their instructions. In order to give them some teeth, an Act of 1669 was passed, introducing a system of Statute Labour, by which tenants and cottars were required to give six days labour with horse and cart, except during time of harvest. Failure to supply the labour rendered tenants liable to confiscation of goods to the value of 30s. Scots. Additionally, powers were given to the Commissioners of Supply to levy a tax on landowners annually of 10s. for each £100 Scots of their land values. Further, the Commissioners could and did use Rogue Money, a rate levied on landowners for maintaining imprisoned vagabonds.

The "Parish Road Days" proved very unpopular and the work performed was of an extremely low order. With the passing of the Turnpike Act of 1751 Statute Labour was set aside and each man over 18 years of age was yearly assessed at a rate of 1s.6d. But since records of births did not exist and baptismal records were often badly maintained or baptisms not recorded at all, collection of the tax was difficult.

We frequently read in Presbytery and Parish Session Minutes of voluntary collections being called for, to erect bridges and repair ferry boats. In the time of the Bishops, 1662-1688, that is from the Restoration of Charles II. to the coming of William III. when the parish of Comrie was in the Diocese of Dunblane, from the Register of the Diocesan Synod dated 25th. April, 1682 we read "Presented to the Bishop and Synod ane Act of H.M's Privy Council in favoures of the burgh of Dunbarton, granting warrand for a voluntarie contribution to be collected throughout the whole kingdom towards the building of ane stone bridge upon the river Leven, recommending to the Archbishops and Bishops to cause the ministers in their respective Dioceses make intimation of the said voluntarie contribution, and to see the same charitablie performed".

In the early days of the Reformed Church, there being an acute shortage of ministers, many parishes were laid to the charge of one. In 1574, the Rev. William Drummond was appointed to be minister of Tullichettle to which were joined for purposes of oversight and preaching, the parishes of Comrie, Crieff, Monzie and Monzievaird. With no bridges over the rivers, his task must have been heavy and often dangerous, albeit he had readers in each parish. Intimation would be made from the pulpit at Tullichettle that the minister purposes preaching in Comrie on the following Sabbath, "gin the river be fordable".

The bridge of Crieff at the Bridgend was built out of the vacant teinds of the parish from 1690 to 1699. An arch of this bridge was destroyed by the retreating Highlanders after Sheriffmuir in 1715. Later the bridge was rebuilt and the work completed in 1868.

On the 17th. January, 1703 we read in the Kirk Session records of the Parish of Comrie that £2. was given "to Alexander M'Nab, boatman, to buy four do alls to mend the boat".

On 1st. September, 1706: "collected for a bridge on Ruthven Water.-£1. 4s".

On 3rd. October, 1708: "given to Alexander Tossoch Boatman in Comrie to help to repair ye boat".

On 19th. June, 1709: "Giv'n to Alexander Tossach Boatman in Comrie to help to repair the boat. He being a poor man.-£2".

A minute of Presbytery reads: "Comrie, June 3rd. 1669- The quilk day being appoynted for visiting the Kirk of Comrie" Mr John Philp, minister of the parish, at the end of the visitation states, "he regraits the want of glass windows, and a bridge, and the want of a churchyaird dyke".

Nothing seems to have been done to meet Mr Philp's complaint about a bridge for we read in a Minute of Auchterarder Presbytery dated 1707, following upon a complaint of the schoolmaster that there were other schools near the kirk, which would, doubtless, make fewer the fees falling to himself, stating, "yet there were waters intervening, which were often impassable, and therefore they did not think fit to make an act to hinder other schools".

During the ministry of Rev. Dugald Campbell, ordained in 1711, estimates were taken on a visit of Presbytery for "the new manse required". It was also proposed next year to build a bridge.

A minute of Presbytery dated April 1st. 1712: "Intimation appointed to be made in all churches of the bounds for a voluntary collection for building the bridge of Comrie, the collection to be brought in to next meeting of Presbytery". The bridge must have been built but a very poor job it must have been, as in 1728, the Rev. Andrew Muschett wrote to one of the heritors, Col. Campbell of Aberuchill that "the bridge of Comrie being in such a tottering case that neither horse nor man can have passage". The good people of Comrie had to wait a long time for a new bridge, dating basically from 1756 or 1770 at a cost of £250—a strongly built stone structure of six large and two small arches with cutwaters, so narrow, "that two empty carts or other horse vehicles cannot pass each other upon it without difficulty or danger". So wrote John Brown, teacher of English, writing and accounts at St. Fillans, and obviously Johnnie Graham agreed with him as, when the bridge was replaced by the present one in 1904/05, he wrote that sweet song with the verse:

> "They said ye were ower nerrow,
> An' no quite up-to-date,
> But mony an awfu' storm ye've stood,
> When Ruchill was in spate".

The Bridge of Comrie is, of course, now called Dalginross Bridge.

In June 1715 Mr. Muschett petitioned for a bridge, probably that at Dalclathick, on the grounds that "one of the charity schools in the parish is like to be rendered inacessible by a rapid stream interjecting between it and the district of the parish from which most of the scholars used to come". He asked for enough of the vacant stipend to make a bridge. The Presbytery directed that application be made to the heritors. The thing done seemingly, for in 1731, as the result of a petition from the inhabitants of Glenartney, the Presbytery appointed a collection be made in the several parishes within their bounds for a bridge over the Ruchill.

The Ross Bridge was constructed in 1792, a short time before the completion of the new road from Comrie to Lochearnhead. Previously to get from Comrie to The Ross, one crossed at Ath nan Sop, entering just to the east of Chattan house and into the Ross, south of what is now Easter Ross. The entry lanes are still discernible and usable. This must have been a hazardous crossing as the Earn flows strong and deep, here.

The Bridge over the Lednock at the east end of Comrie, must have been built around 1799 as John Brown in 1823 writes that it was "a substantial stone bridge-built twenty four years ago". It stood until replaced by the present iron bridge, identical to the Caledonian Railway bridges, and probably built around 1900. Previously, coming from Crieff, one crossed the Lednock near the junction with the Earn, where the waters are very shallow. Of Dalchonzie Bridge Brown writes in 1823, "New Bridge, which in its present state, is just sufficiently broad for one sober pedestrian at a time, and before night!".

Much new roadbuilding was undertaken in the Highlands and Islands by the Commissioners for Roads and Bridges in the early years of the 19th. Century but few petitions to them emanated from landowners in Central Scotland. One of these petitions, if taken up, would have had a considerable effect on life in Strathearn. The plan was for a road from Ardeonaig on the south side of Loch Tay, into Glenlednock and by Comrie to Dunblane by Glenlichorn. The memorial submitted to the Commissioners bears the signatures of Breadalbane, G.S. Drummond, Robert Dundas and Patrick Murray, and is dated 14th. July 1807.

There had for centuries existed over the line of the proposed road, rough tracks usable only for droving sheep or cattle, or by strings of garrons. Wheeled traffic over long stretches was impracticable. A new road would not only have shortened the distance over which folk had to travel, but would greatly assist the movement of raw materials and merchandise. Our district relied for fuel on the peat workings of Monevie, in Glenmaick and in other places such as Glentarken

The Ross Bridge, Comrie, built in 1792.

48

and on the fairly plentiful supply of oak timber obtained after the barking of oak from the extensive coppices in the area. The bark, of course, was exported to the Lowlands for use in the tanning of leather. For those who could afford it, and they would be few, coal had to be moved in panniers slung on the backs of long trains of garrons from the coalmine at Blair-ingone. The increasing use of lime for sweetening grass crops necessitated ever more supplies of fuel, and coal was the ideal fuel for burning the limestone which was now increasingly being quarried in Breadal-bane, particularly near Lechin on north Lochearnside. There was, too, a rapidly increasing population in the district through which the road would pass and ease of access to the south was becoming more and more essential to them.

In 1801 Thomas Telford, probably the greatest civil engineer that this country has produced, was appointed surveyor and later permanent consulting engineer to the commissioners. It was he who surveyed the route from Loch Tay to Comrie and over to Dunblane. Telford greatly favoured the type of farming along Loch Tay with its fine mixture of arable land and its herds of cattle and flocks of sheep. A road open to wheeled traffic would greatly ease the transportation of wool and farm produce to the south and the bringing back of lime and coal. However, as no contractor would undertake the work at a cost less than twice the estimated cost, the petition was turned down in 1811. It is said, too, to have been considered that the route over the watershed at Craiguchdach above Innergeldie, would be too high for winter use. And indeed, it would have so proved, as very much lower down the glen, winter snows frequently block the present road.

However, a notice in the Perth Courier of 1811 reads "Contractors wanted, Road from Comrie to Ardeonaig on South Side of Loch Tay, 6 miles with ten bridges. Plans etc. George M'Farlane, Overseer,

Comrie". It also reads, "contract of second part will be asked for shortly".

This distance would have covered 4 1/2 miles from Comrie to Innergeldie, and another 1 1/2 to above Spout Rolla as far as Bovaine, now submerged beneath the waters of the Lednock Dam. It seems probable that this first part was completed taking, in many places, a very different route from the early unformed track in the glen. The original road from Comrie ran from what is now Melville Square, north through the fields named Acrelands, slightly to the west of Comrie House, into Comrie House Woods and thence out into the upper fields of Lechkin Farm and entering Polyrigg Wood at the sharp right-angled bend near Lechkin Quarry, by a steep ascent to reach the Maam Road to the west of Dunmore Hill where stands the monument to Lord Melville. Descending into the glen the track crossed the slight ford at the foot of the Kingarth Burn close by the Shaky Brig, and turning north west it served the farmtouns of Kingarth, Glaslarich, Tynacroy and Tynashee, and on across the Lednock at Anaba, the Ford of the Cows, where is now a fine stone arch. From thence, the route is the same as the modern one.

The line of the old track is clearly shown on James Stobie's map of 1783. The building of the new road by the two upper fields of Lechkin Farm, Polyrigg and Drumachople (Druim a' Chapuill, or Ridge of the Mare) up and round by Balnasackit (Baile an t-Sagairt, Place of the Priest), perched on a shelf dug out of the precipitous slopes of the Lednock gorge and then blasted round the steep rockface of Dunmore Hill above the foaming waters of the Cauldron must have been a hazardous and arduous task. From here the road follows an easier route crossing the old road leading to the ford and the more modern Shaky Brig, round by a natural amphitheatre facing Kingarth Farm, and keeping the old trackway, still quite visible some hundred yards to its right, to join the old road at the exit from

Tynashee a short distance from Anaba Brig.

With the short extension of the route by a usable roadway from Bovaine in Glenlednock west to Bouachdair, the major portion of the road petitioned for by Lord Breadalbane and others from Ardeonaig to Dunblane was largely completed. The further portion between Bouachdair and Ardeonaig, remained as it does to this day, a track open only to foot passengers and by riders on horseback. The building of Glenlednock Dam and the creation of Loch Lednock has not only drowned the old homesteads of Bovaine, Keplandie and Bouachdair, but has necessitated an alternative route by Glenmaick, and over the saddle into upper Glenlednock and by the Power station to the old track leading over Craiguchdach to Lochtayside. It is further west by half a mile that lies the tiny loch or tarn of Monevie whose peat beds figure so largely in the title deeds of the older homes of Comrie folk.

The Military roads had been built at the expense of the Government and most of the roads in the Highlands and islands by an equal sharing of the cost between Government and the local landowners. The Turnpike Act of 1751 by which the principle of Statute Labour was replaced by yearly assessment on a manhood basis, allowed for the upkeep of the roads and bridges by a system of tolls. Toll gates and toll houses were set up on these roads and a scale of fees for using the road was exhibited on boards set up on the toll house walls. In our district there was a toll at the present Melville Square, with gates for wheeled traffic and flocks of sheep and with turnstiles for foot passengers, on both Drummond Street and in what is now Bridge Street. Older Comrie folk still talk of "The Toll" when Melville Square is meant. There was a toll at the junction of the Comrie/Ardoch Road at the junction with the road by Craigneich to Muthill called Blairnroar Toll. There was another at the junction of the Comrie/Ardoch Road at Mill of Ardoch where the Crieff to Stirling road joins. There was a toll at the east end of St. Fillans where the bridge leads off to the south Lochearnside road. At Dalvreck were two toll bars, one on the Crieff to Comrie Road and one on the road leading off to the Hosh and Glenturret. At the Bridgend of Crieff were two tolls, one on the south Crieff to Comrie road.

These tolls were let out at auction to the highest bidder. From the Perth Courier we learn: "To let: Lochearn Turnpikes. Within the house of Peter Stewart, Vintner, Comrie, on the 7th. day of May, 1811.

1st.   The Bar and Side Bar at Dundurn Bridge.
2nd.   Bar at Comrie and Side Bar leading to Dalginross.
3rd.   Bridge of Turret and Side Bars.
4th.   The Bar near Bridge of Earn (i.e. Bridgend of Crieff) leading to Comrie on South Side of Earn".

"To Let: Oct. 8th. 1812. The Bar near the Mill of Ardoch, the Bar at Blairnroar". "Proposed Bill to Parliament including a road from village of Muthill by Mill of Craigneich to Turnpike Road from Bridge of Ardoch to Comrie.

A branch from Turnpike Crieff to Lochearnhead by Dalchonzie, Aberuchill, Tullychettle or Dabranich (sic) to join at Cultabragan the road from Comrie to Ardoch".

The original track from Comrie to the South by Dalginross as shown in Stobie's map and as is confirmed in its first two miles by Farquharson's Plan of Dalginross of 1767 runs from the Bridge of Comrie to Wester Dalginross, that is roughly where Mid Square now is, then South, keeping Cowden to the East, thence up over the Bogton Braes by Bogton Farm as far as the Puddock Hoose (that is where the road to Mill of Fortune Glentarf and Strowan leaves the present Comrie Ardoch Road). It mounted up to the East of the Newton Rocks by Newton Farm, Bishopfaulds, Culloch, Straid and Cornoch to cross the gently sloping hillside and down into the valley of the Knaik west of the later farm of Langside, thence on by Glenlichorn Farm and skirting the shoulder of Grinnanhill above Braco, turning south west to Kinbuck and Dunblane. The road to Braco which we know today follows a completely different route, touching the old track at no more than a couple of points. This road must have been built around 1810 for we have the notice dated 1811: "The new road from Comrie to Ardoch through Glenlichorn is to be opened in the Summer and will make the carriage less expensive than formerly to those woodcutters and tanners in the South, as Comrie will by then be about the same distance from Ardoch that Ardoch is from Crieff, a saving from 8 to 10 Miles".

The first Tollman in Comrie was Sandy Miller. Sandy was a shoemaker to trade, and had a stated wage for lifting the tolls for the first year, and when the money was got from Sandy it was found that Sandy's wage came to more than what he gave in as the amount collected by him for the toll. The Road Board then resolved to roup the Tolls and give them to the highest bidder. So, when the toll roup came on there were a good many who came forward to bid for them, and Sandy Miller was there with the rest. Sandy was also the highest bidder, and his bid was considerably more than the amount he gave in as collected during the year that was closed. When the Comrie Toll was knocked down to Sandy, the Clerk to the Road Board, looking at Sandy, said, "You expect to do more for the incoming year, Sandy?" Sandy replied that he hoped so. Those who were there had a good laugh to themselves, as they thought that Sandy had a shrewd guess that they suspected he had diddled the Board out of part of the Toll money. Sandy had a brother, named Willie who trained as a "Whip-the-Cat" or travelling tailor. He spent long years at sea and on return to Comrie took up the offices of Letter-carrier and Town Crier. Willie being a strong anti-Protectionist in politics, was in constant conflict with the farmers of the district. He was also a stout Seceder and when the minister introduced Paraphrases in his congregation, Willie did not approve. One Sabbath when the minister began reading the opening verses, Willie turned to his neighbour and asked. "Where is the Psalm?" His neighbour replied that it was the 2nd. Paraphrase. "Weel", said Willie, "you can whistle awa' at your Paraphrase. I'll sing the 23rd. Psalm". And sing it he did while the others were singing the Paraphrase.

The unfortunate Mr. Miller toll-keeper at the lonely Toll at Mill of Ardoch was murdered, probably for the sake of the few shillings taken that day in tolls.

The Toll-bars were the source of irritation and annoyance to all and sundry. They were eventually abolished by the Roads and Bridges Act of 1878, when County Councils became responsible for the care and maintenance of roads and were empowered to levy rates for the purpose. Most of the Toll-houses were taken over by adjoining proprietors at valuation but some went by public roup.

The Toll-house at Melville Square, Comrie became a Newsagents and Stationers shop, which for children seemed, by reason of its hanging racks of papers and magazines, enhanced by the circular shape of the building, to be a veritable Aladdin's Cave. it was owned and run by the family of Mr. Duncan Comrie, Coachhirer for many years. It was subsequently acquired and re-structured by the North of Scotland and Clydesdale Bank.

Until the early years of the 19th. century the traveller to Lochearnhead from Comrie left the village by what is now called Monument Road, and ascending a few hundred yards, turned left off the present Glenlednock road through the "Sheuch o' the Balloch" which separates Willie Bain's Wood from the Craig o' Ross wood and descended into the Glasdale some fifty yards beyond the Ross Bridge, which, of course, was not built until 1792. The line of the old road from there must have been very much that of the present one as it becomes more and more circumscribed by rocky knolls and outcrops.

Certainly, there has long been a usable road as it is clearly described in their beautiful series of Marching Maps produced by the early cartographers Taylor and Skinner, which are described as a "Survey and Maps of Roads of North Britain or Scotland" and dedicated "to His Grace, John, Duke of Argyll, C.-in-C. North Britain, 20th. March 1776". These maps which are in linear form, confine themselves to the roads system of the day, with references to the owners of the various estates through which they pass. They were originally intended for military use and a copy would be carried by the Commanding Officer of each body of troops which passed through any district. They are very finely produced and though limited in their scope, yet contain a wealth of detail.

Our knowledge concerning road conditions and travelling generally, in past times, can only come to us through records and journals of travellers.

In 1771 Pennant published his "A Tour in Scotland", and of our district he records. "Pass by Lars, a seat of Colonel Campbel, agreeably placed amidst woods. On through the village of Comerie, near which are four great stones, erect, and placed so as to form a square. They appear to me the portal of a Druidical temple, or place of worship, now destroyed; and that it was meant to dignify the entrance, and inspire the votaries with greater reverence, as if it was the place of particular sanctity". Were these the stones we see today on the Plains of Tullybannocher of which but two now remain, the others have been removed to make more room for the plough? They were described by the Rev. Mr. McDiarmid as "the large stones at Cluan at the bottom of the Crappich Hills, are supposed to have been a Druid Temple". Or, could they have been the "four-poster" called Dunmhoid close by the cemetery on south Crieff Road.

Pennant continues, "The valley begins now to grow very narrow, being continually intersected by small but beautiful hills, mostly clothed with woods, which occasion every half mile or less an agreeable change of scene; new vallies succeed, or little plains beyond plains, watered by the Earn, here limpid and rapid; frequently to be crossed on genuine Alpine bridges, supported by rude bodies of trees; cver them others covered by boughs, well gravelled over. The higher we advanced the more picturesque the scene grew: the little hills that before intersected the vales, now changed into great insulated rocks, some naked, others clothed with trees. We wound about their bases frequently through groves of small oaks, or by the side of the river, with continued views of the vast rugged Grampians on each hand, soaring far above this romantic scenery. .....At once arrive in sight of Loch Earn, a fine extent of water... filling the whole vale. A pretty isle tufted with trees divides the lake at this end. The boundaries are the vast and rugged mountains, whose wooded bases bound the margin, and very rarely give any opportunity of cultivation. A fine road through woods impends over one side, and is a ride of uncommon beauty. The great rocks that lay above us guarding the lands of Glen-Karken (Glentarken), are most wild and picturesque; for a while bend inwards, then soar precipitous, overtopped with naked rocks, opening in parts to give a view of corn fields and farm houses, at a dreadful height above us..... Return and dine at Comerie".

The present Road from Comrie to Lochearnhead was constructed at the instance of Lord Melville of Dunira. His friend, Sir Patrick Murray of Ochtertyre, kept Dundas informed on the progress of work on his estate of Dunira, its crops and herds, and, also of the progress being made on the new road. On 4th. May 1805, Murray writes, "I inspected the New Road, & I think both the road, & the Dykes on each side of it, very well executed.--The only direction I had occasion to give about the Road, was to break the upper course of Stones a little smaller.--The Contractor has not yet begun to blind it with gravel, nor is all the Metalling broken, & a small piece remains to be formed at the West End.—It will take some weeks yet to finish it. The course of it will be most beautiful. I advised Edington (Lord Melville's Overseer at Dunira), ...that in my opinion the breadth of the Arch over the Boltachan, between Parapets, need not exceed 18 feet, which is the breadth of the New Bridge of Turret. I shall apply to the County for authority to shut up the former Road, altho' such a measure appears almost superfluous." It is recorded that on the 30th. of April, 1805 he was informed that the new road "has been executed on the full breadth required by law in the most substantial manner and in the best possible line of direction at the sole expense of Lord Melville".

At Woodend of Meovie or Tynriach (House of Heath), the road-builders unearthed a number of human skeletons. In the year 1589 Stewart of Ardvorlich had captured some twelve of the Clan Gregor and was marching them east to Perth for trial and sentence. Arriving at Meovie, Stewart changed his mind and caused the Gregarach to be summarily hanged on an oak tree. The bodies were unceremoniously cast into a pit and their place of burial forgotten. With the bones were found metal buttons and scraps of cloth, while the thigh and leg bones were lying across one another. The disorderly state of the remains showed that neither time nor respect had been wasted on their burial. The probability is strong that these were the last remains of the twelve Macgregors.

We learn that "a bridge was erected over the Turret near Eppie Callum's Tree prior to the year 1701, the road down past Milnab being then the principal highway to Comrie and the west. The original road to Comrie crossed the Bridge of Turret and went past the Laggan and Strowan, at the latter place crossing the Earn by one of the old-time narrow and steep bridges".

Dalvreck Bridge over the Turret on the present main road from Comrie to Crieff was built in 1804

D

when toll-gates and toll-houses were also built. In all probability this bridge and roadway figured among the many public works instituted by Sir Patrick Murray of Ochtertyre. Several members of this family at the end of the 18th. and beginning of the 19th. centuries spent much effort in improving the state of agriculture in Strathearn and in opening up of new lines and means of communication. To envisage what travelling conditions were for the folks of Comrie and District from earliest times right up to the early years of the 18th. century, one must look at its topography. At the nodal point of the meeting place of the three rivers we have the Kirktoun of Comrie with its scattering of cottars' homes with their few arable acres behind, its kirk and its school. It lies at the east end of a peninsula bounded on the south by the Earn and on the east by the Lednock. After the narrow pass of the present Glasdale the plain opens out into the wide fields of Tullibannocher and Gerrichrew and Dunira, narrowing again as the east end of Loch Earn is reached.

South of the Earn and east of the Ruchill lie "the barren Moor of Dalginross", Cultibraggan, Cowden, the Lennoch and Strowan.

And again, south of the Earn and west of the Ruchill is the estate of Aberuchill and the smaller estate of Dalchonzie. Further west are the lands of Dundurn.

Running north-west from Comrie is Glenlednock, while westerly runs Glenartney with the Water of Ruchill draining the glen. All of these estates and glens were more populous in the 17th. century than they are today or have been for the past 150 years. Hemmed in by their hills, mountains and rivers, many folks must have lived out their lives without ever leaving the strath. Crofters would travel to market with their few beasts or supplies of oats, some young men would go off to the wars, but it is unlikely that the womenfolk went further than the nearest kirk. Drovers would come over the passes and down Glenogle to Lochearn, or over the hills from Lochtayside to Loch Boltachan where after resting and refreshing their herds they would push on to Port, the modern St. Fillans, across the Earn and into Glenartney by Glen Goinean. Thence they would travel by way of the Carrie and Bealach nam Bo (Pass of the Cows) to Doune and the market or Tryst of Falkirk. Some would travel east by the Earn and Comrie to the market of Crieff and were joined by those coming down Glenlednock from Lochtayside. Pedlars and packmen would come through the strath bringing the latest in goods and news of the great world of the Lowlands. Tacksmen and tenants would pass through performing their "long carriage" dues to their landlords to fetch, in the panniers of their ponies, coals from Bannockburn or Blaringone, and return over the Langside or through the passes of the Ochils.

These were hard and arduous journeys as the hill passes are high and the rivers often in spate. The land, being undrained, was wet and marshy and studded with treacherous mosses. Even today, after three hundred years of improvement, travel can often be difficult. What it was like for our forebears, we can only guess.

To reach Comrie from Dalginross would often be impossible by the ford, when the rivers were in flood. Only by boat would it be feasible and a boat seems to have been kept and a boatman as we read of repairs being done to the boat from the Kirk Session Records of Comrie.

Equally, to reach Aberuchill from the south, from Dalginross, one passed either by the Farm of Blar Dearg (now Tom na Gaske), over the Ruchill and into the lower fields of the Ross; or coming from Crieff by Turret Brig and Strowan Brig, along by the Lennoch and Cowden, one took the old road south of Newton Farm (now Ruchillside) to cross the Ruchill near Old Ruchillside or by Renecroi at the White City and through the Black Wood south of Old Craggish Farm and on to the Pooch Gate and so to the Castle and its environs.

Roads and Bridges

An early road ran from Aberuchill Castle along the south bank of the Earn, by the Dam and Lade serving the Mills of Ross, and further east, almost to the entry leading to the House of Ross, to cross the Earn here into Glasdale at a place long-gone called Widowstoun.

A re-enactment of the droving days. So common in the 17th and 18th centuries to Crieff and after 1770 to Falkirk.

CHAPTER VI

SCHOOLS AND SCHOOLMASTERS

Prior to the Reformation in 1560 all education was in the hands of the Church and its purpose, mainly, was to train young men for service in the Church or in Law. Only those of wealth or social standing were in any position to be accepted for tuition. There was little prospect of training for the "lower orders".

The Reformers, foreseeing the need of an educated ministry and, finding that they were very far from being able to supply a minister in each parish, had one great aim – a school in every parish. As the old Church had from its vast revenues undertaken, among other aims, ministry and education, the Reformers, with much right, considered that a very substantial part of these revenues would accrue to them. It was not to be, however, as the powerful magnates and landed gentry appropriated most of the Church's lands and revenues for their own private purposes. They were the real inheritors of the funds of the old Church and as heritors they became liable to sustain public burdens among which were the building of parish churches and schools and the support of ministers and schoolmasters. It was to be a long time until the dream of a school in each parish was realised. Such buildings as were put up were little better, if at all, than the cots of the rustic poor. At the end of the 18th. century the school at Comrie was described as a "humble thatched village school" while in Glenlednock there was near "the little township of Funtullich..... an old,

Schools and Schoolmasters

thatched, and very primitive school. In winter the children brought peats with them to put on the fire in the middle of the classroom floor. There was no chimney and the peat reek simply found its way out through a hole in the roof." When the first school was erected in Comrie Parish is not clear but we learn from a Presbytery Minute of June 3rd., 1669, taken during a Visitation in the time of the Rev. Mr Philp, that one of the questions posed to him was if he had provision for a schoolmaster. His answer reads, "There was once ane, but not now." By inference there must have been a school and schoolmaster earlier than that date. We find also in "June 1707, on heads of families complaining that the school was not in a central part of the parish, the Presbytery found that there being several glens in the parish, which did not all meet at the kirk, where the school is kept, there could not be a more central place." That there were other schools is evidenced, further, from the complaint of the school-master of the time who was losing income through pupils attending other schools. "The Presbytery found that there were other schools near the kirk, yet there were waters intervening, which were very oft impass-able, and therefore they did not think fit to make an act to hinder other schools."

In the early years of the 18th. century was founded The Society in Scotland for Propagating Christian Knowledge in the Highlands and Islands. This body set up several schools in our area, not all in Comrie Parish. In 1713 they opened schools in Glenartney and Glenlednock; in 1729 at Lochernend which is proba-bly where St Fillans earlier called Portmore now stands; in 1738 at Auchtermuthill, and in 1746 at Glenroar, which we know as Blairnroar.

The numbers of pupils attending these schools at the time of opening were: Glenartney 36 boys and 25 girls; Glenlednock 38 boys and 19 girls; Lochernend 42 boys and 23 girls; Auchtermuthill 66 boys and 37 girls; while at Glenroar were 80 boys and 45 girls.

At the beginning of the 19th. century, the numbers at Glenlednock had grown to about 100. These figures give us some idea just how populous were these glens not 200 years ago and they are reinforced by the fact that in 1820 no less than 80 able-bodied men mustered out of the glen as volunteers.

The various public enactments from the end of the 17th. century show the gradual passing of powers over education from the heritors and ministers of parishes to our present system controlled largely by the State.

The Act of 1696 laid down that the heritors should provide a house for a school and agree a salary for the schoolmaster, not under 100 merks (£5.11s. 1 1/2d) nor above 200 merks, paid in equal portions at Whitsunday and Martinmas, and that each heritor's share should be based on his valued rent in the parish, and that the heritor be allowed relief of half this amount from his tenants for the maintenance of the school and payment of the schoolmaster's salary.

It is clear from the Act of 1803 that the aim of a schoolhouse in every parish had not been achieved as this is again laid down. Schoolmasters must sign the Confession of Faith and be approved by the Presbytery. The heritors and ministers were to fix fees and the schoolmaster was bound to teach such poor children as they recommend. The oversight of schools was handed largely to the ministers while the Presbytery could suspend or dismiss the schoolmaster. The setting-up of schools additional to the parish schools – to be known as "side schools" – was provided for.

The Act of 1838 provided in the Highlands and Islands for endowment by the Treasury of what became known as Parliamentary schools. The heritors had still to provide the schoolhouse but the schoolmaster's salary came out of the funds of the Endowment.

The Parochial and Burgh Schoolmasters' Act of 1861 further increased the influence of the State as opposed to that of ministers and presbyteries. Salaries were raised to a minimum of £35, with a maximum of £80

per annum. Appointment of female teachers was author-
ised and schoolmasters were to be examined by the
Universities instead of by Presbyteries. Schoolmasters
were no longer required to sign the Confession of Faith
of the Church of Scotland, but had to engage not to
teach anything opposed to the Bible or the Shorter
Catechism. Powers of oversight of schoolmasters'
conduct were given to the Sheriff in place of the Presbytery.

The great Education Act of 1872 provided for the
setting up of infant and evening schools and industrial
schools. The Act further laid down in respect of other
schools the duty of every parent "to provide elementary
education in reading, writing, and arithmetic for his
children between five and thirteen years of age."

We learn that the "humble, thatched village school"
of Comrie stood for many a year close to where now
stands the monument to the Rev. Mr McIsaac which
is on the north wall of the Auld Kirk graveyard. There
appears to be no record of its exact location, whether
actually in Dunira Street, or within the bounds of the
kirkyard. Whatever the quality of the building, there
appears to be no doubt concerning the quality of the
work done within its walls. One master was John Drummond who was selected for the post from Campsie
in 1792. His appointment was signed by or on behalf
of the heritors by Donald McIntyre, President of Examiners, John Drysdale for Col. Robertson of Lawers,
James Glass for the Rt. Hon. Henry Dundas and for
Col. Campbell of Monzie, William Brown for Strageath
and Mr Drummond of Comrie, George Ferguson for
John Drummond of Megginch, Donald McIntyre Jnr.,
Donald and Peter Drummond of Balnadalloch.

John Drummond was in addition to being schoolmaster,
Precentor and Session Clerk in the Parish Kirk, which
additional duties with their emoluments usually fell
to the schoolmaster. John Drummond "long and success-
fully taught. In a report of the London Celtic Society
in 1826, giving an account of the parish school, the

names of those who had taken prizes are given. A high eulogium is bestowed on Mr Drummond, whose school is described as having long been the best in the district."

John Drummond died in October 1826, aged 63. He was succeeded by Mr Cameron, a native of Lochtayside and teacher for nearly 50 years. It was during his time that a new school was provided in 1834. This was the school still known to natives as the Old School. Some of the later pupils are still alive today.

The school and adjoining schoolmaster's house were erected by the heritors on land purchased for £230 Sterling from Sir Robert Dundas of Dunira, Bart. The ground is described as "that piece of ground consisting of 57 falls 18 ells scots measure or thereby bounded on the north by the feu now belonging to Archibald McLaren, on the east by the turnpike road, on the south by the common passage or entry from the street of Comrie to the Water of Earn, and on the west by the Water of Earn.... under reservation always of the lock-up house.... with the access to.... and other privileges necessary for the proper use and purposes for which the said lock-up was constructed." The witnesses to this title deed were John Cameron, Schoolmaster in Comrie and Peter Comrie, Vintner, Comrie.

The New School, still in occupation, was erected in 1909/1910. Mr Cameron was succeeded by Mr Gibson and he in turn by Messrs James Goldie, James Murray, James Stalker, William Starritt, Robert Nesbit and Alistair Waterston.

Following upon the Disruption of 1843, a large Free Church Schoolroom was opened on the west side of Dundas Street in December 1845. It closed in 1873 after the passing of the 1872 Education Act. It was taught by Messrs Stewart, McEwan, Craig and Dryburgh.

For many years Mr Duncan Graham had a large school in Comrie and until about 1880 there was, also, a Female Industrial School.

The following minute of the Presbytery of Auchterarder has value as it indicates what subjects were taught, what books were available for the pupils, the aims of the authorities in weaning the people away from Jacobitism, and the eradication of the Gaelic tongue. The Minute reads, "An interesting report was transmitted by the President of the Society for Promoting Knowledge anent the Highland schools within the Parish of Comrie, from which report it appears that there were then three schools maintained by the Society, situated at Glenartine, Glenlednock, and Loch Earn, attended by 53, 66 and 63 scholars respectively; that the branches were the Bible, the New Testament, the Proverbs, Vincent's Catechism, the Shorter Catechism, and other pious books; and that visitors were very much surprised and refreshed to find what proficiency the scholars had made in the branches which they were exercised about. Further the report bears that, having obtained liberty to the boys to divert themselves a part of the day, the visitors, observing them at their diversion, found them punctually obedient to their master's order in speaking the English language and abstaining from the Irish; and there was among the people of these bounds a strong inclination to have their children educated; and the Presbytery conclude with an earnest supplication to the Society not only to continue but to increase their efforts, as a great means of securing the affections of the inhabitants of these countries to our Gracious Sovereign, His Majesty, King George."

The Log Books of Comrie Industrial School appear strangely to modern readers, in some respects. One is struck by the numbers of days' holiday, for example, "No School: pre-Communion Fast." A week later we find, "No School today: Thanksgiving after Communion." or "School dismissed till Wednesday – Old Hansel Monday". There is no mention of Christmas which was still not a Scottish holiday.

Absences through illness are frequent. "Fever raging in the village. Parents keeping children from school."

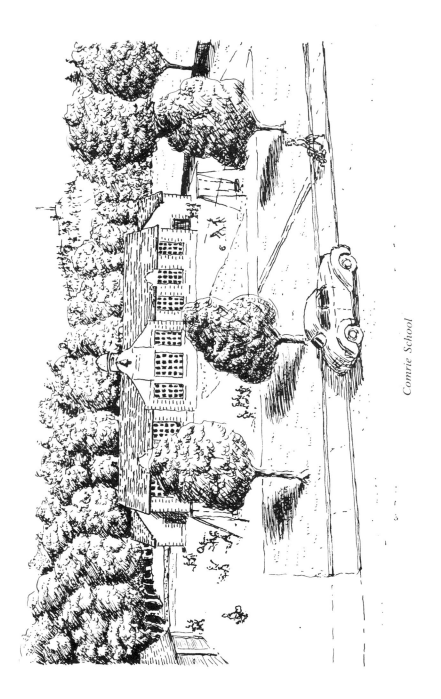

Comrie School

Even animal sickness gave a reason for leave, as, for example, on 30th. March 1866 we find: "No School. Fast in Comrie for Cattle Plague."

The school appears to have been a philanthropic venture, though some small charges were made for attendance. The chief patron is stated to have been Miss Drummond of Drumearn, who was a frequent visitor "to examine the girls' seams." Sewing formed a very large part of the curriculum and some girls enrolled for no other subject. Reading, writing, drawing and singing were taught – Domestic Economy, Physiology and even French were included. There is mention of "Télémaque."

Apart from the frequent holidays much time was lost by girls going off to service, to potato cleaning and hay-making, and working at the oak barking. That children have not changed much is apparent from such notes as, "Could not get some girls in as they were sliding"; "Some girls gone off to gather berries and blaeberries in the woods"; "Found the 2nd Arithmetic class 'Copying'." Sadly, there are frequent instances of "Case of swearing"; "Case of low language. This is a saddening fault here".

Regular examinations were held by the School managers among whom were the Revs. Mr Carment, Dr McDonald, Mr Drummond and Peter Drummond Esq. of Drumearn and by his Majesty's Inspectors of Schools, James Cumming and Alexander Walker. In 1865 Miss Jane Hodge, C.U. started duty as teacher and in 1866 she was joined by Mary Waddell as Pupil Teacher. Miss Hodge was succeeded in 1867 by Miss Elizabeth Gibb and in 1869 by Miss Mary Scott until May 1873 when she received notice from the Managers of the School that in consequence of the altered state of circumstances produced by the New Education Act, of the termination of their agreement.

But schooldays were not over as the school continued as the West Public School, Comrie, the first teacher being Elizabeth Wardrop. A much fuller curriculum was now followed and lessons followed according to the time-table. At the end of her first week the teacher states, "on comparing pupils with those in last school, many of whom worked in the mill, conclude they are exceptionally intelligent and active, more life and fonder of play. Does absence of mill work account for this?". By May 1874 there were 20 boys and 53 girls in the school, but absences through Whooping Cough and fever, probably Scarlet Fever were very common. In January 1873 we read that the school was fumigated twice weekly with sulphur, increasing to twice daily in February. On July 22nd. 1874 we learn that a "little scholar fell into the Earn while trying to get out her slate. Agnes Wardrop (aged 10) fortunately rescued her. Lily Mills was much exhausted and Agnes wet to the neck". Strict rules were laid down with regard to the river and a letter was written to the School Board Clerk about the dangerous state of the river.

Col. Williamson of Lawers was the chairman of the School Board, and in November 1874 he "kindly ordered gas brackets and meter". Miss Wardrop was evidently a conscientious teacher and something of a disciplinarian. On January 1875 we read "Two new boys causing irritation among boys. Obtained father's leave (McCallum) and brought them into subjection". However, the teacher kept an eye on the boys for on January 22nd. and on February 12th. we read "McCallum boys work well".

Miss Grace McNaughton is reported as "doing well at her work as Pupil Teacher - quiet and regular", and later "continuing to do well - attentive and obliging to the children".

On February 14th. 1876 Elizabeth Ann Wardrop sent in her resignation which took effect from April 1877 and was succeeded by Mrs Mary Salter. The Government Report on March 1876 stated. "The school passed a very creditable examination in all standards. The Grammar, Geography, & History were good and the children showed good intelligence generally. The older pupils had been well drilled in the first year's course of English Literature and Physical Geography. The offices are not in good repair and part of the playground is very wet and muddy".

Grace McNaughton passed well under Art 19 (c). P Brough. Clerk.

In October 1877 Miss Mary Macpherson entered on her duties as certificated teacher.

The work of the school continued with high praise from examiners and inspectors but there are many complaints regarding irregular attendance by reason of children being employed by farmers and others at potato–lifting, by removals at term time and by heavy snowstorms.

In February 1880 the roll had declined to 46 pupils and on the 25th. of that month, the West Public School was closed and the two public schools were amalgamated.

CHAPTER VII

DUNIRA

The estate is today greatly shrunken from what it was in the days of the man who was primarily its creator—Henry Dundas, Viscount Melville, Baron Dunira.

The lands had originally been part of the immense possessions of the Perth family which had been sequestrated after the abortive rising of 1745. The Earl and titular Duke of Perth, like all of his family for generations, was a Jacobite and confirmed supporter of the Stuart cause.

Henry Dundas came of a family which for centuries had been among the more important members of the landed classes, the family's origins can be traced back to the twelfth century and throughout the years its leading members were strong supporters of the kings of Scotland. One branch of the family settled at Arniston in Midlothian in the 16th. century, and it was from this branch that Henry Dundas descended.

As did many of their class in Scotland, the Dundases entered the lucrative ranks of the legal profession, and many of them rose to the highest positions in Scotland. And like so many in such positions of power and influence, they did not hesitate to further the fortunes of their kith and kin and of their friends. They carried nepotism to its highest pitch.

Robert Dundas, fourth laird of Arniston and father of Henry Dundas, was born in 1685. He became Solicitor General for Scotland in 1717 and lord Advocate in 1720. Dismissed by Walpole in 1725 for opposing the Malt Tax, he became one of the leaders of the Scots Opposition in the Government. His influence in legal affairs and in Parliament made him a powerful force in both Scotland and at Westminster. In 1737 he was accepted again into Walpole's favour and became a judge of the Court of Session. His son, Henry, by his second wife, was born in 1742.

Robert Dundas, having become President of the Court of Session in Edinburgh, took steps to have his eldest son appointed to each office which he himself vacated as he rose higher in legal position. This son acted in similar manner toward his younger brother, Henry, who at the early age of 21 was called to the Scottish Bar. Three years later, Henry entered the Government as Solicitor-General for Scotland, though he had passed no legal examinations at Edinburgh University, nor even contested an election.

By a fortunate marriage to Elizabeth Rannie, the wealthy heiress to the estate of Melville Castle and to a fortune of £100,000, Dundas set himself on the way to great influence and power. (Fifteen years later she left him, but he kept both the castle and the fortune.) He forced his election into Parliament as member for Edinburgh County and later of the City of Edinburgh which he represented from 1774 to 1802.

Dundas was now well on the way to those high offices of state which were to win for him the nicknames of "King Henry the Ninth" and the "Uncrowned King of Scotland". He was well-liked and efficient. Strangely, in Parliament, though the English members had no love of the Scots and their 'outlandish' speech, he retained to the end his Scots tongue and accent, which by an odd paradox greatly influenced his English colleagues.

As Lord Advocate for Scotland he had the decision on which Scottish Representative Peers should have seats in the House of Lords. He also chose Tory candidates for election to the House of Commons. The sinecure position of Lord Privy Seal he gave to himself at a salary of £4,000 per year.

Already immensely powerful north of the Border, he was now Pitt's foremost colleague in Scotland. He became Secretary of State of the Home Department, President of the India Board of Control, Secretary of State for War, Treasurer of the Navy and First Lord of the Admiralty.

Beneath the Prime Minister, there was no more powerful statesman in Britain, and that at a time when the country was at deathgrips with the armies and navy of France. Wellington and Nelson were both grateful to him for his exertions and to him are owed many additions to the British Empire.

In Home Affairs he did much to improve conditions in factories and mines and finally had the shackles of "slavery" striken from off the miners who for centuries had been in a position of abject submission, tied as they were with their wives and children to the mine owners.

In 1803 he was created first Baron Dunira and Viscount Melville.

Two years later, in April 1805, the brewer, Samuel Whitbread brought into the Commons a motion that Dundas was guilty of malversation, accusing him of having misused a million pounds while he was Treasurer of the Navy. The actual work of this department was carried out by a Paymaster, appointed by the Treasurer. The Paymaster was another Scot by the name of Trotter, who did himself well from the job. Dundas's signature alone was sufficient for vast sums of money to be paid over and once he allowed Trotter to use a million pounds of public money for private purposes of speculation. Having achieved his ends, Trotter returned the million to the Navy Office.

The motion in the House of Commons was passed by the casting vote of the Speaker, and Melville, recently enobled, elected to be tried by his peers. This was the last case of impeachment in British history. Before the official enquiry he and Trotter saw to the burning of all important papers, ledgers and accounts in the Navy Office. These accounts dealt with 134 million pounds of public money though there was no suggestion that Melville had helped himself to even a hundredth part of the amount.

Ten charges were brought against Melville in June 1806 before the House of Lords. The Tory Peers, many of whom were indebted to him for favours and sinecures, acquitted him on all charges. But, he never again held public office and his days of power were over. He was later reinstated as a Privy Councillor.

It was remarked at the time of the trial that "it was hardly the thing an honest man would do.", while William Wilberforce felt compelled to write that "Dundas was a loose man; yet he was a fine fellow in some things. People have thought him a mean intriguing creature, but he was in many respects a fine warm hearted fellow."

The truth is that Dundas was no better and no worse than very many others of his class and time. Corruption, nepotism and bribery were endemic in high places. That Dundas should be any different from his fellows was not to be expected.

Dundas was well-acquainted with the delights of Upper Strathearn. He had many friends among the local lairds, perhaps more especially the Murrays of Ochtertyre. When the Law Courts and Westminster were in recess, he would stay at Ochtertyre and engage in shooting parties, out after the moorfowl or grouse. At a later stage, when he had obtained the estate of Dunira, Sir Patrick Murray of Ochtertyre was his confidant and adviser on agricultural affairs and, when he was at a distance, acted almost as his agent in keeping him abreast with the progress of work on the many schemes he had undertaken at Dunira.

Dunira and the surrounding district, were part of the forfeited estates of the Drummond family, and at this time were administered on behalf of the Crown by the Commissioners for the Forfeited Estates. It must have been through their agency that Dundas took a lease of Dunira House and the shootings. Here he would withdraw from the hurly-burly of affairs to the peace and quiet of the beautiful countryside.

Robertson, in his exhaustive 'General View of the Agriculture of the County of Perth', writes, "Duneira is a singular place. The scenery from Crieff to Lochearn, a distance of 10 or 11 miles, is in the highest degree romantic and delightful. It is called by travellers the Montpelier of Scotland. Duneira is the most diversified place of the whole. Ochtertyre and Lawers are discovered by passengers with ease. They present themselves to the eye. The valley before them is wide and the mountains more distant: but the situation of Duneira shows it to be a retreat from public business and the bustle of the world. There the valley begins to narrow, as you look west; and you approach the foot of the rugged Grampians: the mountains before you seem to be closing from both sides, and to stretch up their towering heads to the clouds. The magnificence of these mountains, and the richness of the scenery of Duneira are obvious to all passengers, but there is one feature of it, very uncommon in a mountainous country, which does not immediately attract the attention of every passenger: I allude to the extent of the low ground of Duneira and Tullybannocher, which unite and form a horizontal plane of 629 acres."

"In July 1778 Dundas travelled north from London, intending to spend a shoot at Oughtertyre for a fourth-night and settle some family business with Sir William Murray. In Perthshire he had also business with the Drummond family, whose Earldom of Perth was forfeited. The family was in debt and Dundas came to its assistance, behaving with a delicacy which made him appear 'to receive an obligation, in place of conferring one'. His motives were, perhaps, not wholly altruistic. Among the Drummond possessions was the estate of Dunira on the River Earn, and Dundas's acquisition of this delightful place later, seems to have been bound up with the Drummond family's indebtedness to him, and with the restoration of the forfeited estates, in which his interest now revived and which he was instrumental in affecting four years later".

It was about 1784 that Dundas first acquired land at Dunira and in 1787 he brought in a motion in the House of Commons that the Highland estates forfeited after the '45 be restored to the original families. Generally, the bill which followed was approved and passed without opposition. The measure in itself was wise and liberal, and from it flowed much goodwill towards the Government, and not least to Henry Dundas.

He was so satisfied with the beauties and potentialities of the estate that he set about its enlargement by buying additional farms around, Meovie, Woodend of Meovie and Gerrichrew from the Drummonds. It appears that the late proprietor of the estate promised to let Dundas have these lands, and James Drummond, to whom the estates had been restored, aware of the family's debt to Dundas, carried out the agreement, on the understanding that if Dundas should ever sell, the family should have the option of repurchase. At a later date he purchased the estate of Comrie which lay between the village of Comrie and his property of Dunira. His holdings now stretched from the river Lednock on the east to St. Fillans in the west, and from Craig Odhar in the north to Glenartney in the south. This compact area of land Dundas set about to improve with great energy and enterprise. Sadly this 'improvement' was not accomplished without hardship to the small farmers and crofters who became victims of the 'clearances' which in this district had their early examples about 1762 on the Drummond Estates during the jurisdiction of the Commissioners. The village of Comrie from being a scattered community of smallholders congregated around the kirk as it had been for centuries, now, at the end of the 18th. century began to take the shape it has today, when many of the 'sma' folk' took up feus and set themselves up as cottage weavers. Many of the crofts and farm-touns whose names appear on early maps now begin to disappear--Belna, Meovie, Ballinluig, Cochladow and many others, while even the Neolithic standing stones at Tullybannocher were reduced to two, to enable the plough to be worked more expeditiously. It is impossible to say now just how many such relics of the past were destroyed because they impeded agriculture.

Dundas, now the complete country gentleman immersed himself in his farms and woodlands, in draining and fencing, in treeplanting and regular cropping of the great stools of oak coppice. The sale of oak bark for the tanning industry was valued at £4,000, from Pollyrig Wood on Glenlednock Road and from the Fichead Sgillinn, now the Twenty Shilling Wood on the St. Fillans Road just west of Comrie. (This latter is still known to local people as the Twenty Pence Wood. The name probably has reference to the land measure of Twenty-penny land but the local tradition is that this was the payment for a day's work at the oak-barking).

One of Dundas's early tasks on Dunira was the building of a new house. He had previously occupied a small cottage on the banks of the Earn which was so small as to allow of only one married couple being put up at a time. Simultaneously he started on the ambitious scheme of diverting the course of the Boltachan Burn which ran through the Gerrichrew Farm for a distance of over a mile to join the Tullybannocher Burn, and was responsible for much of the flooding which turned the land into little better than a morass. The Boltachan was diverted to run in a north to south direction from Dunira House to the Earn. The condition of the improved farm land was beyond measure and land which was worth no more rent than 15/- per acre was now valued at £3 an acre. Much draining was done both on Dunira and on Tullibannocher where in 1808, 5000 roods of draining were completed.

New farm buildings were put up in both places, at Dunira, stabling for eight horses, a byre for twelve cows, two pig houses, poultry house, barns, cart sheds, and a thrashing mill driven by water. In addition, he built a two-storied house for his overseer and five homes for farm servants. All were built substantially of stone and lime and roofed with blue slate.

Much building of roadways and foothpaths was accomplished throughout the estate together with miles of stone dykes--a task of immense labour, the stones for them being uplifted from the surrounding farmland. Such is their quality that still today they stand almost without repair or alteration.

The day-to-day oversight of farming and forestry operations was in the hands of the grieve, Alexander Edington, whose emoluments were £50 a year plus house, cow, meat and fuel. He stayed with Dundas until the latter's death in 1811.

As one of the leading landowners in the district, he took a full and active part in all local matters. At his sole expense he had the road from Comrie to Lochearnhead rebuilt from its miserable state on the latest principles then applied to roadbuilding, and while in London in early 1805, was informed that the new road had been completed. The oversight of this work was largely in the hands of Sir Patrick Murray of Ochtertyre whose family in those years did so much for the improvement of the countryside and convenience of the populace in constructing roads and bridges in West Perthshire.

It may be that both Dundas and Sir William Murray were instrumental in having the Ross Bridge built in 1792 and Dalchonzie Bridge a few years later. The latter bridge and that at Dundurn were partly constructed from funds supplied by the Forfeited Estates Commissioners.

As one of the chief heritors he enquired into and had regularised the position and stipend of the parish minister of Comrie, and took a local census of the population. When the rebuilding of the Parish Kirk became necessary in 1803 through its being in a state

Dunira House

of advanced disrepair, Dundas took his full share with the others, and when these did not give a favourable response to his suggestion "that a steeple at Comrie would be a great ornament to that part of the country", he undertook to contribute £100 extra himself, in addition to what he might be liable for on his assessment. The church was opened for worship in 1805 and is today the Youth and Community Centre or "The White Kirk". He had built, too, at Comrie House, a weir across the Lednock which supplied power for a sawmill, a meal mill and a weaving mill. Later the water powered the distillery which for many years stood at Lednockbank and it may be that the wheel now at Dunira Sawmill, where the realigned Boltachan enters the Earn, and which is the last working water wheel on the Earn, came from here.

Henry Dundas, Lord Melville, filled his days to the full in national and local life. He died in 1811 and the following year his many friends in Perthshire erected to his memory the 72 feet high obelisk on Dunmore Hill. It is of Glenlednock granite, quarried at Innergeldie. There is another great pillar and statue to him in St. Andrews Square in Edinburgh.

The general layout and amenity of the estate is very largely the work of Lord Melville, but much, too, was accomplished by his successors the Dundas family of Beechwood, whose Sir Robert purchased the estate from the second Viscount Melville in 1824.

A new house was built in 1852 by Sir David Dundas, to the east of the old house. It is built of Bannockburn freestone carted from Greenloaning station. The farm steading was erected in 1879 and many workers' cottages. A new garden of 4 1/2 acres was laid out together with glasshouses, vinery and peach-house. Larch, spruce and oak coppice were planted to about 1500 acres in extent. The bed of the Boltachan Burn and the Tullybannocher Burn were causewayed to stop sudden flooding while 35 miles of footpaths, roads and numerous bridges were constructed.

The Melville Monument on Dunmore, Glenlednock. Erected in 1812 by his friends in memory of Henry Dundas, Viscount Melville.

Dunira

The Dundases of Beechwood and Dunira were much respected in this district. They have their private burial ground in the woodland directly opposite the accommodation bridge leading to Kindrochat Farm.

After being in possession for a century, the Dundases disposed of the estate to Mr Gilchrist Macbeth in the early 1920's. They retained part of the Comrie estate and made their home at Comrie House where the last member of the family died in 1982, within a few short weeks of his one hundredth birthday.

Mr Macbeth died at the end of the Second World War and his widow disposed of the estate which has since largely been broken up into small parcels and sold.

Mill wheel at Dunira saw mill at junction of Boltachan and Earn. This wheel was originally at one of the mills at Millside on the Lednock. The last working wheel on the Earn.

CHAPTER VIII

THE MURRAYS OF OCHTERTYRE

The founder of this ancient family was Patrick, third son of Sir David Moray of Tullibardine. The family name remained as Moray until William, the third baronet, changed it to Murray. Patrick received as his patrimony the "Dry Isle" of Ochtertyre and the lands of Dollerie. On what was once an island but is now a peninsula stood Castle Cluggy, now in a ruinous state, but obviously once it had been of great strength, being 20 feet in height with 5 foot thick walls, and internal dimensions of about 17 by 18 feet. It is said to have once belonged to the Red Comyn and in about 1460 was described as an Antiquum Fortalicium. When Bruce laid waste the countryside after the discovery of the plot against his life by Lord Soulis, Patrick de Graham and the Lady Joanna, daughter of the then Earl of Strathearn, he made an attack on Castle Cluggy.

The castle possibly dates from the 12th. century, and may have been built after the battle fought in 1003 on the adjoining Plain of Monzievaird to the south of the loch, between Malcolm II and the usurper Kenneth IV. Kenneth was slain and his body taken for burial to Iona.

During the reign of Charles I, plague ravaged the district. To the west end of the loch is a large mound marking the burial place of the victims from the district of Monzievaird. By Act of Parliament in 1645, public contributions were directed to be collected for the starving, plague-stricken inhabitants of the parishes

of Crieff, Monzievaird and Comrie. The Keeper of
the Public Magazine of Perth was ordered to give
out fourscore bolls of meal for the use of the three
parishes. In addition, voluntary contributions were
to be sought in the parishes in Perthshire which had
been by-passed by the plague.

From an early date there existed bitter animosity
between the Murrays and the Drummonds, the former
being unwilling to sit under any control by Drummond,
Steward of Strathearn. This led to a bloody conflict
and savage act of vengeance in 1490, in the reign of
James IV.

In 1203, King William the Lion confirmed the gift
made by Earl Gilbert of Strathearn to the church of
St John of Inchaffray and the Austin canons serving
there, of the church of St Serf of Monzievaird, in free,
pure and perpetual alms. About 1490 the Abbot of
Inchaffray ordered the collection of teinds of the
Drummond lands possessed by the Murrays, and there
was dispute as to who should collect them. The teinds
were exacted by force. Lord Drummond was absent
from Drummond Castle and his eldest son, William,
Master of Drummond, gathered his clansmen around
him and marched to Ochtertyre. The opposing forces
met on Knockmary on the south side of the Earn, near
Crieff. The Drummonds were worsted and were retreating towards Drummond Castle when a large reinforce-
ment joined them of M'Robbies from Balloch and Campbells under Campbell of Dunstaffnage, who were in
Strathearn to avenge the murder of Campbell's
father-in-law, Drummond of Mewie, who had been
killed by the Murrays. The now strengthened Drummonds
set off after the Murrays who, with their wives and
children were giving thanks for their success in the
old kirk of Monzievaird. Tradition says that they might
have escaped notice had not one of their number fired
an arrow from a window. Their assailants speedily
set fire to the kirk, and as its roof was of heather
thatch, it was soon consumed and all within, save for

one member of the Murray clan who was saved from the flames by a Drummond. This Drummond fled to Ireland and on his return was rewarded by the Murrays with the farm of Drummondernoch. Confirmation of the destruction of the people was found much later when foundations were being dug on the site of the old kirk for the Ochtertyre mausoleum, and great numbers of bones of the victims were found.

Such was the horror created by this awful deed that James IV, despite his friendship with the Drummond family, arrested the Master of Drummond and many of his accomplices, had them tried, found guilty and executed on the Gallows Hill of Stirling.

Though Ochtertyre was the main family home, they lived much at Fowlis Easter. This property was acquired by William, who was created first baronet of Nova Scotia in 1673, and was a member of the Scots Parliament. Patrick, the second baronet, lived for lengthy periods at Fowlis and the family commuted between Fowlis and Ochtertyre by way of Bullion's Boat over the Tay, north of Perth. They travelled by lower Glenalmond, Buchanty and Monzie. Much of their time was spent in hunting pursuits, coursing of hares being the chief sport of the time. They used hawks to kill muirfowl and Glenturret was noted for its fine breed of falcons. (A pair of falcons presented to George III at his coronation by the Duke of Atholl, as token of his tenure of the Isle of Man from the Crown of England, was taken from the Blue Craigs or from the cliffs of Ben Chonzie.). The use of traps and snares was one of the chief means of supplying the table. Pigeons, too, figured largely on the table. There are no doocots now remaining in Upper Strathearn, but doubtless there were several in the 17th. and 18th. centuries, with their flocks of birds, which caused great loss to the grain crops of the poor tenantry.

A strange deed of entail was executed in 1726 by Patrick, the second baronet, to the effect that no heir to the title was to take a title above baronet under pain of Forfeiture.

Another strangeness in the family is that a Patrick succeeded a William and a William a Patrick in unbroken succession for many centuries.

Patrick, having married a daughter of the Haldanes of Gleneagles, had kindly ties with the folk of Auchterarder and did much for the poor tenantry burnt out of their homes by the order of the Earl of Mar when marching to Dunblane and Sheriffmuir in 1715. The folk had remained loyal to the House of Hanover.

Sir Patrick was one of the four Perthshire members in the Last Scots Parliament and recorded his protest against the Union with England in 1705 and again in 1706. After the Revolution, no Murrays were Jacobites, unlike their neighbours and longtime enemies, the Drummonds.

The fifth baronet, Sir William, served in the Army but retired early to devote himself to agriculture. He was the first to introduce modern methods of husbandry to this area, very largely through the application of lime to grassland. So fine were his crops that other farmers soon followed his example. A rich source of marl lime was found in the sediments of Ochtertyre Loch which was extracted by means of a dredger and carted away by what is still named the Marl Lodge, on the Comrie to Crieff road.

Towards the end of the 18th. century, Sir William had built the present mansion house of Ochtertyre.

In October 1787, Burns, on his Highland tour, stayed in the old house, prior to the building of the new mansion. He reported, "I lived, Sir William's guest, for two or three weeks, and was much flattered by my hospitable reception... I find myself very comfortable here, neither oppressed by ceremony nor mortified by neglect." In company with Miss Euphemia Murray of Lintrose, cousin of Sir William, Burns walked up Glenturret where he was inspired to write the piece, "On scaring some water-fowl in Loch Turrit—1797". —and in praise of his companion, the sweet verse—

"Blythe, blythe and merry was she".

Sir Patrick who succeeded in 1800, took a large part in public business and held many high offices. He was an excellent gardener and by judicious planting of trees and woods, he inspired the neighbouring lairds to beautify and enrich their grounds. It is largely to him and his example that we owe today so much of the beauty of this district. He was the founder of the Strathearn Agricultural Society which gave a lead to landlords and tenants in greatly improving the quality of their crops and herds.

It is to Sir William that we owe the many fine highways and bridges in Strathearn, most of which were constructed in the early part of the 19th. century. He was a great friend and confidant of Henry Dundas, Viscount Melville of Dunira, who often shared his shooting parties and was greatly indebted to him for advice in farming matters. When Melville was absent from Dunira on State business, his friend maintained a lengthy correspondence with him at the time when Melville was building up what was almost to be a model estate at Dunira. Regular reports were sent by Sir Patrick on such matters as the realigning of the Boltachan and Tullibannocher Burns, the construction of farm buildings and, of greater interest to the public, the making of the new road, at Melville's expense, from Comrie to Lochearnhead.

Sir Patrick's brother, Sir George, had a distinguished career as a soldier and statesman. His army career culminated in his appointment as general in 1841. From 1820 until 1832 he was Member of Parliament for the County of Perth, and it was during this period, in 1829, that a petition from over seventy intending emigrants from the parish of Comrie, was presented to him requesting that he make approaches to the Governor General of Upper Canada on their behalf for grants of land concessions. The petition was sent forward and the request granted, for in the same year these Comrie emigrants sailed to Quebec aboard the brig Curlew. Sir George died, full of years and honours in 1846.

Sir Patrick, the sixth baronet, was followed by Sir William, who, on his first marriage to Helen Margaret Keith, assumed the name of Keith Murray. Although he held the position of Colonel of the First Perthshire Battalion of the Militia almost until his death, his interests lay rather in music, the arts and in astronomy. In 1852 he had erected a splendid observatory to the west of the mansion, and installed two fine telescopes, the largest of which, when the observatory was dismantled, was gifted to the University of Glasgow, where it was known as the "Ochtertyre Telescope". (It is of interest to note that here in 1884 was recorded the lowest barometric pressure ever recorded in Britain, 27.33 inches.) He was a man of the widest interest in the people of the district, whom he often invited to view the stars through his instruments and to attend the concerts he frequently held in his house, and to wander at will through his extensive grounds.

Sir William was succeeded in 1861 by Sir Patrick Keith Murray, who emulated his father in public generosity and community spirit. The lovely grounds were open to all and even boats were supplied freely for the inhabitants of the district to use. He proved a kindly laird to his tenants and to the folk of Crieff. Perhaps his greatest gift to Crieff was that of a public supply of water from Loch Turret, without which the town would not have risen so early to become the favourite holiday and tourist resort that it became.

Sadly, in more recent years, the estate has fallen on ill times. The lands and shootings have been sold, as has the mansion house and the beautiful loch. The final curtain fell a few years ago on the tragic and untimely death of Sir William. So, the Murrays are no more at Ochtertyre.

CHAPTER IX

ARDVORLICH

The Ardvorlich Branch of the house of Stewart had a Royal origin in Robert II, King of Scots. His second son, Robert, Duke of Albany, whose line supplied Scotland with Regents and virtual rulers for over fifty years but was cut short in its third generation by their execution at Stirling by order of James I – that is all, save one, Sir James Stewart, who took refuge in Ireland where his natural son, James Beag was born and who returned to Scotland where his aged grandmother, Isabella, Countess of Lennox, sometime Duchess of Albany, gave him a grant of land at Baldorran in Stirlingshire.

The "Baldorran" family later moved northwards and one laird, William, got a lease of the Lordship of Balquhidder, becoming Royal Baillie. He was the founder of the clan of Stewart of Balquhidder and his successors, the Stewarts of Ardvorlich, claimed and at times exercised the chiefship of that clan. William's sons and his kinsmen received grants of land in the district, and since at that time surnames were being first used in the Highlands, many local inhabitants took the name of their landlords, the name of Stewart. This was the foundation of the clan. It was about 1582 that Alexander Stewart, son of James the last of Baldorran, settled at Ardvorlich, where his descendants are to this day, the last remaining lairds in this part of Upper Strathearn still in possession of their ancient patrimony.

E

Ardvorlich

Situated as they were on the very edge of the High-lands, beset on all sides by powerful neighbours – Camp-bells of Argyll and Breadalbane, Drummonds of Perth, the warlike Macnabs of Glendochart and the landless MacGregors, – they were still united and strong enough to fend off their foes, and on their own part make predatory incursions into the richer Lowlands, when they felt the need to increase their herds of cattle and to pay off old scores against those who had preyed upon their lands.

The estate of Ardvorlich, in terms of highland estates generally, is but a small one – for more than four hundred years, as it is to this day, only about seven thousand acres. It lies just to the north of the Highland Line, where the Grampian Range borders the rich Lowland plain. On the North it is bounded by Loch Earn and to the South rears up the great summit of Ben Vorlich which faces the South front of the house. The land is mountainous in the extreme and there is but little arable land in the haughs by the lochside.

To the East lies Ardtrostan which forms part of the great Drummond Estates; to the West is Edinample, once a stronghold of the Campbells of Glenorchy who became Marquises of Breadalbane. The castle was built at the end of the 16th. century and with Finlarig at Killin and Balloch, later Taymouth, at Kenmore completed the southern defences of Breadalbane.

Over the summit of Ben Vorlich the mountain drops down into the Dubh Choirein, part of the extensive Forest of Glenartney, long the possession of the Kings of Scotland and later of their ardent supporters, the Earls of Perth.

The scenery along the lochside is truly Highland, with steep declivities strewn with bold rocky outcrops and mossy boulders. Thickets of hazels abound among the fern and bracken. A striking feature by the roadside is the great stand of 200 year old larches, grown from seed brought from the larch plantations of "Planting John" the Duke of Atholl, who imported the seed from the Austrian Tyrol.

As Royal Baillies of Balquhidder the Stewarts had no easy or peaceful office to fill. The original owners of the land were the Clan Laurin, who had come from Dalriada. There were three chiefs of the clan, Conon of Balquhidder, Maurice of Tiree and Laurin of Ardveich. Ardveich lies on the north shore of Loch Earn, almost opposite Ardvorlich. Supporters of Kenneth III at the Battle of the Standard, the name of Laurin of Ardveich, Lorn de Ardebechey, none the less appears on the Ragman Roll of 1296 when, doubtless for political reasons rather than through conviction, the chief swore fealty to Edward I of England.

The Maclaurins were stout and loyal allies of the Stewarts of Appin and took to the field with them in mutual support down to the abortive '45 rising. Like so many small highland chiefs who held their land by the sword, they never took charter to their lands and in the end, were completely dispossessed by those who did, and so along with the other small clans of Balquhidder, the MacIntyres and Fergusons, they lost their holdings.

Meanwhile in Balquhidder the star of the MacGregors was rising towards the end of the 15th. century. At the Battle of Auchleskine the MacLaurins were being worsted by the Buchanans of Leny and they called on some MacGregors for assistance. This was given, but at a bitter price to the MacLaurins, namely to hand over the right they had always had to be the first to enter the Kirk of Balquhidder. It was into this scene of internecine strife that, about 1500, William Stewart entered as tenant of the Crown and Baillie of Balquhidder. As the MacGregors became more powerful, so the strength of the MacLaurins declined. In 1532 Sir John MacLaurin, Vicar of Balquhidder was killed within the precincts of the kirk during a brawl.

The chief of the MacGregors at this time was MacGregor of Glenstrae, but being a minor, he was under the tutelage of Duncan Laudasach MacGregor. Duncan was a man of savagery and bloodthirstiness who by his misdeeds, forays and murders led the MacGregors down the road to eventual retribution and final proscription. About 1550, Duncan Laudasach, or Laideus as he was sometimes called, fell upon the homesteads of the MacLaurins in Balquhidder under cloud of night, and slew 27 of them, men women and children. Harried by the chief men of the district, Duncan and his two sons surrendered to Campbell of Glenorchy at Finlarig whence they were taken down the loch to Balloch at Kenmore to the "heading pit". With most men's hands against them, deprived of their lands and homes the MacGregors were in piteous plight. Only Queen Mary seems to have realised the root cause of their lawlessness - namely that they were landless. Everywhere they were subject to eviction - "They cannot live without some rowmes and possessions" she said, and requested Menzies of Rannoch to allow them to settle in Rannoch. She issued a general pardon to the clan, remitted all past offences and received them into the Royal peace. However they continued to be harried by Grey Colin of Glenorchy and by his son, Black Duncan of the Cowl. The chief, Gregor MacGregor was beheaded at Balloch in 1570.

While the MacGregors of Rannoch and Breadalbane were continually feuding with the Campbells of Glenorchy, the MacGregors of Balquhidder had their own feud with the Drummonds of Glenartney and Strathearn. Drummond of Drummondernoch, Keeper of the Royal Forest of Glenartney had summoned the clan for 'hership and reif'. About the year 1588, John Drummond in pursuit of his duties, came upon poachers killing deer. He had their ears cropped and sent them on their way as a warning to others, that poaching in the King's Forest would not be tolerated. They returned home and showed their wounds to their kinsfolk. Shortly later, came the retribution for the indignity put upon their clansmen, apprehended in what was considered a very honourable occupation - deer poaching.

In the autumn of 1589, King James VI being about to marry Anne of Denmark, planned a great feast at Stirling and to that end instructed Drummondernoch to fetch supplies of venison from Glenartney Forest. Unluckily, he was alone when he came upon some of the Children of the Mist. They killed him, and severing his head, set off home with their bloody trophy. They headed for Balquhidder to join up with their own clan to find shelter among other desperate men. They must have followed the old drove road through the Bealach Gliogarsnaich and down Glen Vorlich to Ardvorlich, probably well-knowing that the Stewart laird was married to the sister of Drummondernoch. Alister Stewart was away from home at the time and the Lady of Ardvorlich, hospitality being a first duty of the age, asked them in and set them at the table. While she left the room to obtain food and drink for them, the unwelcome guests unwrapped the bloody head from its plaid and set it upon the table and filled the gory mouth with bread and cheese. The Lady of Ardvorlich returned bearing the food and saw the dreadful sight of her brother's head upon the table. She completely lost her reason and dashed from the house, great with child as she was. She took to the hills and the woods, and after many days gave birth to a child near the little loch on Beinn Domnhuill which to this day is called, Lochan na Mna, or the Woman's Loch. On his return home, Ardvorlich organised his men to search the hills and glens, but it was only after the women at the summer shielings reported that their cows were giving little milk, that he found that his

N.B. At a later date (circa 1800) Sir John Macgregor set about trying to lay the blame for the murder on the Glenco men, but there is no doubt it was the MacGregors.
A sept of the MacGregors were known as "The Clan Duilcheach" or the "Children of Dougal of the Mist".

demented wife was stealing the milk to feed her infant. Persuaded to return home she was a long time in regaining her reason.

Meantime, the murderers, terrified at what they had done, fled to the protection of their chief in Balquhidder. Hither the young chief, Alasdair MacGregor of Glenstrae, assembled his clansmen, and placing the severed head upon the High Altar he set his hand upon it, and swore that he would take the blood-guilt on his own head and never reveal the names of the murderers. Each clansman in turn swore likewise.

Soon the news reached the government in Edinburgh and the Privy Council resolved that they must be rid, finally, of this nest of thieves and assassins. On 3rd. February 1590, "the Lords of Secret Council, being credibly informed of the cruel and mischievous proceedings of the wicked Clan Gregor, sa lang continuing in blood, slaughters, *herships, manifest reifs and stouths," outlawed and condemned the entire clan for the murder of Drummondernoch.

A commission was issued to Huntly, Atholl, Argyll, Glenorchy and others to "seek, tak, and apprehend" MacGregor of Glenstrae, his immediate kin, and over a hundred of the clan named in the commission, together with "all others of the Clan Gregor or their assisters, culpable of the said odious murder, or of theft, reset of theft, hership and **sorning." They were to be tried on the spot, and if found guilty were to be executed forthwith, their possessions being forfeit, half to the State and half to whoever arrested them. They were to be pursued with fire and sword.

The Drummonds and Stewarts of Ardvorlich being most closely affected by the murder of Drummondernoch, were among the first in pursuit of the Clan Gregor, but it was Campbell of Glenorchy who was to prove their most bitter foe.

* plunder, spoliation and theft.
** sorning: taking food and lodging by threat.

The MacGregors, driven to desperation, defended themselves with resolution. Harried out of their homes they took to strong places in the hills. Lord Drummond and Ardvorlich entered Balquhidder by surprise and slew every MacGregor they could lay hands on. The wretched folk took to their ancient place of refuge in the wilds of Rannoch. Harried here by Black Duncan of Glenorchy they sheltered their wives and children in Atholl where they were given protection in the house of Blair itself. The MacGregors were eventually received into the King's peace and pardoned for the murder of Drummondernoch. They were still without lands of their own and at the mercy of any who might have a grievance against them. And being without means of support, they had no option but to resort to their old habits of theft and marauding. In 1603, together with their allies they made a great raid into the Lennox where they slaughtered some eighty men in Glenfruin, nearly all of them being Colquhouns. Their huge creach numbered 600 cattle, 800 sheep and 280 horses. This was too much for the King and Council in Edinburgh, and by an Act of April 1603, their very name was abolished. There was to be no guilt attached to any who slew a MacGregor. It was forbidden to shelter or protect them – they were nameless and landless.

These were dangerous times, too, for the Stewarts of Ardvorlich. Their lands and cattle were as open to raids by mischievous caterans and thieves as were those in the Lowlands. In 1620, one such raid on Ardvorlich took place when a party of MacDonalds of Glencoe attempted to harry the House of Ardvorlich. This raid was beaten off and some seven MacDonalds were slain and lie buried by the Brig of Ardvorlich on the lochside, as a stone erected at a later date bears witness.

A little space further down the loch stands a similar memorial stone which from its type and inscription would lead us to think that it was set up at the same period as the MacDonald stone. It bears the curious wording - "This stone marks the place of interment of Major James Stewart after removed to the family vault at Dundurn, died about 1660." This James Stewart may have been the son born to the Lady of Ardvorlich after her harrowing experience in seeing her brother's bloody head on her table, brought there by the "Children of the Mist". If he were that son much might be explained for his murderous behaviour after the Battle of Tippermuir in 1644, when the Marquis of Montrose with his Royalist army routed the forces sent against him from Perth. In his army were young Lord Kilpont, son of the Earl of Menteith and his close friend, James Stewart. After the battle, while the army rested at the Kirk of Collace, some quarrel appears to have broken out between the two friends which ended in Stewart dirking Lord Kilpont. Several differing reasons are given for the quarrel. Was it because Stewart accused Kilpont of treachery in that the latter had been ordered by the Estates to lead his forces against Alastair MacDonald's Irish invasion in support of Montrose, but at Buchanty before Tippermuir, had turned his coat and thrown in his lot with Montrose? Or was it because Alistair MacDonald, in marching down Loch Earn to join Montrose caused much damage and loss to the property of James Stewart, who, planning to exact repayment, informed Kilpont of his intentions and that he treacherously exposed these plans? However it was, James Stewart fled to join the forces of Argyll, Montrose's bitter enemy, and subsequently was granted pardon by act of Parliament in 1645.

Despite his tempestuous life, James Stewart lived on for many years and died in his bed at the age of 85. But the world had not yet done with James Stewart. His kin and clansmen gathered to his wake and funeral and started for the burial at Dundurn. Half way there they were informed that his enemies were waiting in ambush for the cortege, intending to dishonour his corpse. Hastily digging a hole by the lochside, they "shoughed him in", and later when times were more peaceful, dug him up and interred him in the family burial vault in the chapel of Dundurn where his father and his successors to this day lie buried.

Robert Stewart of Ardvorlich, though of Royalist sympathies, like many of the small lairds with leanings towards the Jacobites, decided against involving himself or his folk in the Rising of 1715, though his brother took up his sword for the Old Pretender. Again in 1745, when he was an old man for his times, having been born in 1680, Robert stayed quietly at home. In so acting, he, in all probability, saved not only his life and liberty, but his lands and possessions.

But if Robert's life at home was quiet and peaceful his was never an easy situation. His lands of Ardvorlich marched on the east and south with those of the Drummond family, the Earl of Perth, a stauch Jacobite, whose estates were sequestrated after the '45, and on the west with the Campbells of Glenorchy, who became the Breadalbanes, and were for the Government. And further west in Balquhidder on land which had once belonged to the Stewarts, there had been baptised on "7th March, 1671, Donald MacGregor in Glengyll parish of Callander upon the certificate of the Minister thereof and Margaret Campbell son baptised Robert." This was the famous or notorious Rob Roy whose exploits during the rest of his lifetime must have caused concern to the Ardvorlichs as they did to so many lairds, both great and small. However, this is not Rob's story, save to say that his depredations in Western Perthshire and Stirlingshire in his justifiable vendetta against the Duke of Montrose, kept the entire district in a state of turmoil and drew the attention of the Law to the immediate neighbourhood, thus adding to any local troubles the Ardvorlichs may have had.

Life, thereafter for the Stewarts would follow a quiet path. They had little of this world's gear and their living must have been almost as spare as that of their clansmen on what was not a highly profitable estate. Their fortunes revived during the 19th. century when many members of the family served "John Company" in the army of India.

In our time Ardvorlich is still the estate and home of the much respected laird, Major 'Jock' Stewart, who lives the life of a quiet country gentleman, home again after years of service in the Black Watch in France, North Africa and Italy.

Above: Ardvorlich House, Lochearnside. The lands here have been in the possession of the Stewart family for 500 years.

Left: Stone by roadside near entrance to Ardvorlich House on South Lochearnside.

CHAPTER X

THE ESTATE OF LAWERS

The line of possession of the estate of Lawers, Strathearn, cannot be clearly shown without tracing the name of the estate back to its original, namely, Lawers, Lochtayside.

For over two centuries the senior cadet branch of the Campbells of Glenorchy, were the Lairds of Lawers, Lochtayside, the first laird being John, son of Sir Colin Campbell, first laird of Glenorchy. John Campbell, who was styled "of Auchreoch", was killed at Flodden. Lawers had been gifted to Sir Colin in 1473 by James III, in gratitude for his assistance in bringing to book, the murderers of his grandfather, James I in the Blackfriars' Monastery of Perth.

The second laird, James Campbell and his spouse, Margaret Forrester, obtained a charter of the lands of Fordew, Glentarkane and Balmuck in January 1526 from John Drummond, who became a member of the Order of Friars Dominican, and had held these lands in hereditary fee, his mother, wife of Sir William Drummond of Kincardine, had held in liferent. The second son of James Campbell, John, was styled "of Fordew", now Fordie.

The third laird of Lawers, John Campbell was knighted at the coronation of Queen Anne, wife of James VI and I in 1590. His second son, Colin, had a charter of Aberuchill on 12th. July 1596. He it was who had the castle built in 1602. (It would be of interest to learn that the ancient, badly weathered stone in the kirkyard of Comrie is that of the true builder of the castle. Its inscription reads "John Forbra, maister masoun in Aberuchill, ane honest man, died 1602"). Colin was the founder of the family of Campbells represented today by the Campbells of Kilbryde. The sixth son, John, secured a charter of the town and lands of Clathick in 1628 from John, Earl of Perth. He was styled of Ardeonaig, Innergeldie and Clathick.

The sixth laird of Lawers, in financial difficulties, made over the Barony of Lawers with his other lands on Lochtayside in 1657 to George Chrystieson and James Russell, Master of Cowan's Hospital, Stirling. His son, James the seventh laird, held the estate in name only.

It is said that when the Lochtayside lands were sold, earth was brought from Lawers to Fordew in Strathearn, which was afterwards designated "Lawers". Colonel Campbell of Lawers was a warm friend of the Protestant cause, and held command of a regiment of the Reformers. His successor, Sir John, was knighted by James VI in 1620, and having married Margaret, Baroness of Loudoun, in her own right, was created Earl of Loudoun in 1638. As Chancellor of Scotland, he opposed the arbitrary measures of Charles I and was so strongly opposed to Cromwell that he was excepted out of the Act of Grace, but pardoned in 1654. At the Restoration, he was deprived of the Chancellorship, and fined in the sum of £12,000 Scots. His brother who succeeded him, equally opposed Cromwell, raised a regiment to oppose the "Protector", but was defeated at Inverkeithing with heavy loss. His son and heir fell foul of the Clan Gregor. Determined upon vengeance, the clan attacked Lawers House one midnight, intending to murder Colonel Campbell. Just as they were about to kill him, he begged to be led to the little chapel in the park to say his prayers. This was allowed, but on the way to the chapel he induced his captors to accept a ransom of 10,000 merks, to be paid at the inn in Balquhidder on the following Monday. Colonel Campbell duly appeared with the money, but a troop of cavalry he had secretly ordered to surround the inn, captured the brigands, who were later taken to Edinburgh and publicly hanged.

The chapel referred to stands in the park just to the south of the mansion in a grove of yews. Only the east gable remains with a double panel on the outside. There is no device or inscription. The chapel was once the burial place of the family of Lawers. The double line of fine oak trees between the roadway and the Earn may have been planted as an embellishment to the chapel, as they are much older than the mansion house. Somewhat to the west, and south of the public road, an irregularly-shaped field, now scarcely discernible through the loss of its boundary trees, is named the "Bellman's Acre". For ages this field was part of the payment for the services of the Bellman at the chapel. The bell, bearing the date, 1519, was given to the Kirk of Amulree by Campbell of Lawers about 1751.

Colonel Campbell had a distinguished career in the Army, during the campaigns of Marlborough and later at Dettingen and Fountenoy, where his leg having been shot off, he died in 1743. It is said that he had spent only one night in the remodelled house he had built in 1738 to designs by William Adam. The original house had been a simple, plain Scots mansion.

In 1784, the estate was acquired by General Archibald Robertson, and in 1813 it passed to his niece, Miss Boyd Robertson who married her cousin, David Robertson Williamson, a judge of the Court of Session, under the title of Lord Balgray. The estate at this time was of very considerable extent, and covered about 50 square miles of country, including all the land from Innergeldie, along the east bank of the Lednock to Lawers, and over the watershed into Glenalmond. The very distinctive circular sheep pends with high stone walls in these areas are typical of the Lawers estate.

Lord Balgray did much as an 'improving' landlord

Lawers House: Imposing Palladian mansion remodelled in 1738 from a design by William Adam.

to beautify and modernise its agricultural potential. Sadly, in so doing, he broke up many small holdings and rased mills and dwellings, and dispossessed the long-time tenants. The mill at Milton was one such pulled down about 1815. The miller, old Peter Cram, and his wife and family had to move into Comrie where they worked as weavers, and finally, in 1820, emigrated to the Beckwith area of Upper Canada, where so many folk of Upper Strathearn took up their 100 acres holdings in the early part of the 19th. century. An examination of the population figures for Glenlednock will show how great was the decline in the number of people. The very names of their habitations are passing even from local memory. Small heaps of stones and ruinous lime kilns, with their dykes of stone and feal, and the primitive trackways, are the silent memorials of the folk who scratched out a living up and down Glenlednock, as they are of the days of "Improvement".

On the death of Lord Balgray's widow, Colonel David Robertson Williamson, her grand-nephew, succeeded in 1852. He, too, was a great improver and spent vast sums of money, around £50,000 in building model workers' cottages, and in drainage, roadmaking, planting of fine trees, and in fencing the estate to keep the sheep from wandering. On one farm alone, Innergeldie, thirty miles of fencing were erected.

Despite his many eccentricities, concerning which stories are still current among natives of Comrie, Col. Williamson, though a thorough autocrat, not only promoted many schemes to improve agriculture, animal husbandry and forestry, often to the benefit of his neighbours, but also took a great interest in the welfare of the people of the parishes of Comrie and Monzievaird.

For many years he campaigned to have the railway extended from Crieff to Comrie, but met with much opposition from landlords through whose lands the line was planned to run. He finally succeeded and the line was built, and the station of Comrie, on his land at the Laggan, was opened to trains on 1st. June

1893. It had originally been planned to run the line along the south bank of the Earn and the station located in Dalginross, but the laird of Strowan vigorously opposed the idea.

On the occasion of his golden wedding, the people of Comrie and District put up the small obelisk which stands on a rocky eminence between Tomperran and the Milton. The former house, which had previously been the Land Steward's house, became the home, after his father's death, of his only son, The Rev. Father Williamson who had been banished from Lawers during his father's lifetime, having been converted to the Roman Catholic faith during his student days at Oxford. It was Father Williamson who converted a row of cottages, curiously named "The Transvaal" on the west bank of the Lednock near the bridge, into the small Chapel of St. Margaret's. It is interesting that he brought to Comrie three Irish Catholic widows with their families, two of whom he lodged in Coneyhill. From beneath that roof came two Bishops of their Church, Bishop McGee of Dumfries and Galloway and Bishop Foylan of Aberdeen.

Huge tracts of lands were disposed of at different times and are now held by other landlords.

CHAPTER XI

ABERUCHILL AND THE ROSS

In considering the estate of Aberuchill as it once was, and the origin of its name, we must look, not at the location of the castle alone which is very far from the mouth of the Ruchill, but at the whole promontory including The Ross itself, far back to the march with the Forest of Glenartney. The bounds are the Altanish Burn which separates it from Dalchonzie and Dundurn, the River Earn and the Water of Ruchill. There are two exceptions from this compact area of land. From the Altanish Burn to the Aberuchill Burn south of the Earn, a few acres delineated by a now fast-disappearing ditch belonged to Tullibannocher across the Earn, while the eastern fields of Craggish Farm towards the junction of the Earn and Ruchill once belonged to Dalginross Estate. This latter boundary is clearly shown on the Aberuchill Estate map of around 1790, and is corroborated by Farquharson's plan of Dalginross of 1767, which, curiously, shows "an old thorn tree" as one of the boundary markers.

Since the mid-1800's and into the 19th. century small parcels of land have been sold and carved out of the eastern extremity of Aberuchill. We shall consider these later.

The name Altanish is a corruption of Allt Tamhaisg, the burn of the Ghost or Spectre, though why, none now knows. The water is sparkling clear as it flows over a bed of broken slate which used to be quarried high above. The great spoil heap on the face of the mountain stands out clearly. Slate was also quarried near the march with the Forest and many older homes in Comrie are roofed with Aberuchill slate, probably the first slate used here when the use of bracken and heather was discontinued. The quarrymen were bothied at Tomanoir. Quarrying was discontinued in mid–19th. century when the estate was purchased by the Dew-hursts, wealthy thread manufacturers from England. There is a tradition that when Queen Victoria visited this district, she stopped her carriage and had a draught of Altanish water which she pronounced as being the sweetest she had ever tasted.

In 1596 Colin Campbell, son of Campbell of Lawers, Lochtayside, obtained a charter of the lands of Aberu-chill from the Crown, James VI then being on the throne and not yet translated to his more desirable residence in London. Like most of his Stewart ancestors, James was addicted to the chase and the nearby Royal Forest of Glenartney was well known to him, as would the lands of Aberuchill and Strathearn, generally. In 1602 Colin Campbell had his tower house, the central portion of the present castle, built. The architect and builder would appear to have been John Forbra (or Forbes) whose tombstone dated 1602 lies in Comrie Auld Parish Kirkyard. He is described on the stone as Maister Masoune in Abbiruchill, "ane honest man", and from his name perhaps one of the great Aberdeenshire castle builders of that time.

There are many fine examples of their work in that county, when the need for some comfort and elegance had overtaken the need of absolute defence. The addi-tions to the building on the east and west are the work of the Dewhursts.

The Campbells were shortly created baronets, possibly Baronets of Nova Scotia. The Crown being chronically short of money, the Earl of Stirling, founder of Nova Scotia, to finance the colony, sold on behalf of James VI and Charles I the newly created dignity of Baronet. Every Baronet created in Scotland from 1625 to 1707 was a Baronet of Nova Scotia. To save the new baronets the trouble and difficulty of taking seisin of their new land in Nova Scotia, a legal fiction declared that part of the esplanade of Edinburgh Castle should henceforward be declared to be Nova Scotian territory. By stepping within this pale, the new Baronets satisfied the laws of Seisin or Sassine, having paid the requisite sum of 3000 merks for their dignity.

A later member of the family, Sir James, assumed the legal title of Lord Aberuchill when he was a member of the Court of Session in Edinburgh. A strong supporter of the Hanoverian Monarchy, yet living close to the equally strong Jacobite family of the Drummonds, after the Revolution of 1688, Sir James in 1693 petitioned Parliament "for reparation for the serious losses he and his dependents had suffered for their unflinching adherence to their political principles, and from the raids of the rebel clan of MacGregor". Parliament decided that his losses amounted to £17,201 Scots. However, instead of paying him in cash, Parliament passed an act granting him the privilege of holding annual fairs in five different places round about, including one of "the burgh of Inveruchill" a name which has now disappeared.

In 1692, Sir James Campbell, Lord Aberuchill, was one of the judges at the infamous trial in Inverary of James Stewart of the Glen. This was the case of the Appin Murder when Stewart was sentenced to death for the killing of a Campbell factor, by a jury and bench that were packed with Campbells. No one today believes that he had anything remotely resembling a fair trial.

In 1704 the Campbells disposed of the estate to James Rutherford, an Edinburgh advocate, who married Mary Drummond heiress of Strageath and took the name of Drummond of Comrie. During his tour of the Highlands, while staying with the Murrays of Ochtertyre, Burns paid a visit to Aberuchill and recorded in his journal that he had had a cold reception. The private burial ground of the Drummonds lies moated and walled in a sad, mournful wood not far from the west entrance to the castle park. Close by stands the now far decayed King Oak and in the adjacent park, the Queen Oak. They are called the Royal Oaks of Strathearn and are said to have been planted by a Scottish king and queen. In their prime they must have been grand specimens. Nearby the Queen Oak is a slight hillock which is named Ardvorlich's Knowe, though even the late Laird of Ardvorlich, Major "Jock" Stewart could suggest no reason other than the two families had been friendly and that some trees from Ardvorlich may have been planted on the knoll.

The Drummonds were among the early Improvers. The great drainage canal from the meadow west of Craggish Farm, running from the Pooch Gate, in front of Craggish House and taking a sharp right-hand bend east of the disused Railway Bridge and along by the fields of The Ross to enter the Ruchill near its junction with the Earn, is clearly shown in the Estate map made around 1790. The packhorse bridge over the canal still stands, indicating the very old road from Dalginross by Blair Djarg Farm, now Tom na Gaske. The dam, Aberuchill Dam, on the Earn must be of the same date to supply water to what was then called the New Mill, now the Mills of Ross. Two lades here powered two mills one of them a saw mill. The later owners, the Dewhursts, who acquired the estate in 1853 being thread manufacturers, had need of a large supply of bobbins and many were made here, giving the name Pirn Mill by which name it is still locally known. Great acreages of oak plantings for coppicing were created, especially that wood known as Ross Wood. Oak bark was a valuable commodity and added greatly to the revenues of the estate.

Access to the castle and estate in early days and for long afterward was never easy as both rivers, the Earn and the Ruchill, had to be forded, which could have been hazardous in time of spate, to which the

Ruchill is especially subject. There was a considerable population immediately adjacent to the castle where they could seek protection in time of strife, as the aforementioned map gives evidence. There were for long farms high up into the hills above the castle at Carshalton, whence came the Miss Macfarlane who much later about 1880 left the money which built the handsome Free Church. Close to Carshalton were the farms of Blairmore and Craggan Soleir, which even in the days of the Rev. Mr James Carment who died in 1882 were subject to his catechising visitations. (It is interesting to notice that on leaving Glendochart, Archibald Dewar having the Quigrich in his charge, removed to Blairmore, either as a tenant or cottar. He subsequently went to Canada in 1818 taking the Quigrich with him. With the Dewar family's agreement, the holy relic of the Celtic Church was returned to Scotland in 1876. It is now in the National Museum of Antiquities in Edinburgh "for the use, benefit and enjoyment of the Scottish Nation"). Between the Castle and Carshalton lie Tomanoir and Montellie, both of which were homes of the Macnaughton family whose later members still live in Comrie. Downhill from Blairmore is the farm of Dalrannoch, built originally as a shooting-lodge and lower still, in its nook, the Cuilt.

Now down on the flat level of the Strath we reach the once great dark pool of Linn e Chullaich, now rapidly filling up with gravel. The great stone embankment was built after a mighty flood in the late twenties which tore away a great bite from the north bank and destroyed the roadway. We soon cross the Cuilt Burn which like all such streams into quite modern times was alive with sea-trout, for which Upper Strathearn once had an enviable fame. On the left is the Black Wood and at the corner a triangular space known as the White City. Here the tinkers and travelling people once set up their tents, McDonalds, Campbells, McPhees and many others. If they stayed for any

Aberuchill Castle, the central tower-keep was built by Colin Campbell, son of Campbell of Lawers, Lochtayside, in 1602.

length of time as they used to be able, their bairns attended Comrie School and despite their hard lives, were good scholars. The White City, too, was the entrance to a ford over the Ruchill into Dalginross by a farmtoun named Renecroi to the old roadway by the farm of Old Ruchillside and Cowden.

At the edge of the Black Wood stands, now deserted, the old farmhouse of Craggish for long inhabited by the Morrisons, it is said for some three hundred years, until they moved further down to Drum an t-Sogail, the Ridge of the Rye, at the head of the Ross road. Returning a few hundred yards we come to the eastern entrance gates to the Castle policies and Craggish House, the dower house of the estate at one time, and now sadly demolished farmhouse of Craggish Farm, known originally as Ross Farm. The very distinctive building has been removed to make way for modern buildings more in keeping with intensive and mechanised farming.

The one-time village of Ross was once a fairly populous place with separate statistics published along with those of Comrie and Dalginross. The cottars were largely engaged in weaving and dyeing and had their bleaching greens along the west bank of the Earn. The fields running down to the Ruchill were known as The Acres and each household had a few fields, originally on the run-rig principle, but about 1790 these were largely set out in kenches or cavels, which system was more favourable to the tenants.

With the building of the Ross Bridge in 1792 and that at Dalchonzie, movement of folks and goods was greatly eased. The old fords from Chattan corner and that crossing the Ruchill to Blair Djarg Farm, that east of the Mill of Ross to Glasdale, and that at Dalchonzie fell into disuse. Travel became not merely easier but very much safer.

The eastern portion of Aberuchill estate now began to be sold off and small estates created. The first was that of Drumearn, bought by Peter Drummond who had made his fortune in Australia. What had been a boggy marsh was drained and fields and woods laid out and a very fine mansion built. This house after being in several hands is now the Abbeyfield Home. Mr Drummond was greatly involved in good works in Comrie and was one of the supporters of the Industrial School which trained many young girls in homely tasks. He had built the Free Church in St Fillans and allowed the erection of the quaint and historical Earthquake house in his grounds. On a minor scale, he gave the cottars of the Ross access to what is called "the Bog" for the digging of clay, "for the maintenance of their buildings".

Somewhat later, Dr and Mrs Melville converted what had been a row of cottages into the handsome property of Rossbank, now Easter Ross. About 1908, Mrs McLagan built the House of Ross and rebuilt it after its destruction by burning by the suffragettes in 1914. Auchenross was built by the Balfour-Melville family somewhat later. The row of houses for letting known as Glenview was a re-creation from old cottages by David Carmichael in 1907. He was one of three brothers, builder sons of Samuel Carmichael, whose firm is still active today.

Aberuchill Estate is now understood to be owned by an American Oil Syndicate for sporting purposes, and the rearing of pheasants is now on a large scale. Access for the folk of Comrie may be somewhat restricted. If this is so, it will be very sad as during a long lifetime, they were not merely not denied, but even welcomed. Who would not wish to view the daffodils blowing in the springtime, if nothing else?

CHAPTER XII

THE CLAN NEISH OR MACNISH

The traveller through St. Fillans views as he passes the east end of Loch Earn, a small, low, stone-strewn island—its name Neishes' Isle, once a strong place of the small Clan Neish. Nothing about this tree-clad island suggests that here an appalling massacre took place, resulting in the virtual extinction of the clan.

Without doubt, the island is artificial in origin, a crannog, having been a place of refuge and defence in Stone Age times. It is connected with the lake-shore by a low causeway, under water level. Approach to it can, and could, only be made by boat. Doubtless, the occupants made sure that theirs was the one boat near the east end of the loch. Indeed, there is a record that at Linlithgow, in 1490, in the presence of James IV and his Council, John, Lord Drummond undertook to "within 15 dais fra this day furth to ger cast doon ye house of ye Ester Ile of Loch Ern, and distroy ye strenthis of ye samyn, and tak away ye bate, and put her to ye Wester Ile."

From the 13th. century, the Neishes were in possession of various scattered lands in Upper Strathearn. The castle, or rather, "strength", on the island would be their principal place of refuge in times of trouble with their stronger enemies, chiefly the MacNabs of Loch Tayside and Glen Dochart. Their lands in Strathearn, after the fall of the once powerful Celtic Earls, were greatly coveted by envious neighbours. Much of the land was granted in fee to royal favourites, such as the Drummonds and Murrays, and gradually, the Neishes, who like so many Highland clans had no charters to their possessions, were ousted and, as land-holders, disappear from Strathearn.

In 1480, Brice Neish was a tenant of the King in the lands of Easter and Wester Dalgarus, now Dalginross, and his widow, Mariot in the same year became tenant of Easter Dalgarus and Drummenerenoch which was set to Master Alexander Inglis, Dean of Dunkeld, who was bound not to move the tenants, among whom was Mariot, relict of the Neisch.

Sadly, the Neishes became involved in the feuds between the Drummonds and the Murrays and there is a Bond of 1492 by Lord Drummond and Sir William Murray of Tullibardine, anent their feud:- "And if the wife and bairns of umquhile Brise Neson will come and remain at the Tack of Ester Dalgarous that it be restored to them, they paying the grassum of the terms to run, as is above written; and as for the rest that they remain still with their tacks that they are now in."

In 1501, Donald Neissoun (or Neish) had his part of Easter Dalgarus let to John Murray of Strowan. The Murrays, like others of their ilk, speedily obtained Crown charters of the lands they procured. In 1510, John Murray of Strowan received a charter of Strowan, Wester and Easter Dalgarus, and Easter Glentarf. Drummenerenoch was afterwards granted to one of the Drummond family. The tribulations of the Neishes between the upper and nether millstones of Drummonds and Murrays were as nothing compared with the enmity between them and the MacNabs of Killin.

The MacNabs were long established around Killin on Loch Tay and in Glendochart. They were a fierce, warlike people who engaged in battle with most of their neighbours. As the Clann an Aba, children of the Abbot, they feuded with the Dewars of Strathfillan concerning the relics of St. Fillan. The Dewars success-fully upheld their rights and obtained a charter confirm-

St Fillans at the east end of Lochearn. The island is Neish Island where the Neish family was massacred by the MacNabs of Killin about 1612.

ing them in possession, and their troubles with the MacNabs faded away. The MacNab feud with the Neishes was long drawn out, and many minor skirmishes ensued, the most disastrous for the Neishes taking place in about 1522 at Glen Boltachan. The Glen and Loch of that name lie roughly due north of St. Fillans. In later centuries, there was an extensive commonty here, where the cattle drovers from Breadalbane rested and restored their herds on the way to Doune and the Tryst of Falkirk via Upper Glenlednock and Glenartney. The MacNabs carried the day and the Neishes lost their chief and most of their fighting men. Those who escaped were reduced to being mere freebooters who preyed on travellers along Loch Earn. Finally, about 1612, they carried their depredations too far and at Christmastide, waylaid a party of MacNabs returning to Killin by Loch Earn from Crieff, laden with supplies of Christmas cheer. Retiring to the island stronghold, they withdrew the only available boat and made merry in their home. Finlay, seventh chief of the MacNabs, decided that finally he must rid himself of the thorn in his flesh. Cryptically, he addressed his seven sons, men of great strength and courage, "the night is the night, if the lads are the lads." Uplifting a boat from Loch Tay, the sons crossed the hills and came down by Glentarken, and crossing Loch Earn, arrived at the island. All unsuspecting, the Neishes were holding high festival. The door was soon broken down, and rushing in, the MacNabs slew all within, save for one lad who managed to hide. Taking the head of the chief and carrying their boat well into the hills where they tired of its weight and abandoned it, they returned to Killin, where they greeted old Finlay with their grisly prize. The remains of the boat were still visible in Glentarken until the early 19th. century. There are occasional glimpses of Neishes in Strathearn from the 17th. to the 19th. centuries, but, as a clan, their power for good or ill was gone.

CHAPTER XIII

THE MCGROUTHERS OF GLENARTNEY

The McGrouthers, over a lengthy period, were occu-
piers, as owners or tenants of various farms and crofts
in Glenartney and Blairnroar, an extensive part of
the great domains of the Drummond family, the Earls
of Perth. There is mention of one, Gilawnene McCrouder
as a witness to a charter granted by Patrick de Comry
to John de Comry in 1447. The Comrys for long acted
as servitors and stewards to the Earl of Perth—they
are sometimes called of Comry and sometimes of
Ross. In all likelihood, the McGrouthers were also
some sort of officials in the Earl's household, and at
different times were tenants or tacksmen on Drummond
farms. For centuries they were settled in Achinner,
Dalchruin, Dalclathick Mill, Lednaskea, Straid, Craigneich, called then Innerclair, and more especially at
Meigar. Of this last-named they were the proprietors,
and of some considerable areas around Trian. They
were clearly of some standing locally, as at different
times they married into the families of Stewart of
Ardvorlich, Drummond of Drummondernoch, and the
Murrays of Strowan. That they were of fairly affluent
means is evidenced by their advancing money to James,
Lord Perth and to William, Viscount Strathallan.

As adherents of the Drummonds, ardent supporters
of the Stuart cause, they suffered not a little in following their laird, during the 17th. and 18th. centuries.
Living in a fairly small geographical area, they were
all probably of the same basic family, though settled

on widely scattered holdings over the years.

It would appear, too, that the MacGrouthers of Maryland in the States are descendants of Alexander MacGrouther of Craigneich, Glenartney, as he named one of his holdings, "Craigneich". Three brothers of the name were present at the Battle of Worcester in 1651. James was killed, and Alexander and John transported to America as indentured servants. Having "tholed his assize", Alexander took up land in his own right.

The following peremptory letter, so redolent of the days of heritable jurisdiction, was received by William McGrouther in Dalclathick: "William McGrouther in Dalclathick, you are hereby ordered to acquaint William McNiven in the same town, and Alexander McGrouther in Dalchrown to goe along with you as officers to command the company of our men that is to come out of your glen, and all the men are hereby ordered to obey your commands on the highest perrile, which you are to intimate to them as you shall be answerable to us, and this shall be your warrant. Given at Drummond Castle, the fifteenth day of August, 1713. (Signed) Drummond.

"See that none of the men of whatever rank of Achunner be absent as you shall be answerable to us, and all the men in good order."

William McGrouther may be the same person as the William Cruder, subaltern in Logie's Regiment, who was taken prisoner at Preston. If so, he must have later been pardoned and returned home, for in the Kirk Session Minutes of the Parish of Comrie, of which kirk the McGrouthers were among the heritors, we find this entry:

1747. "An Accott of the reparaition of the Kirk Loft of Comrie & what money was laid out for the same.

Imprimis William M'Gruther of Meggar for repairing the flooring of the Loft and Loft Door paid five pounds, seventeen shillings, four pennies

Scots money August or September 1747 years. As his proportion for his seat in the Breast of the Loft South Side."

An earlier minute of the same Session Book records:

1709. 24th Nov. "The Session considering that the people concerned in the loft in the west end of ye kirk are desirous that the menner of its division among them be registrate that all debates in after ages about it might be prevented, the samine was agreed unto which is as follows. The South Side of the Loft belongs unto the persons following. The first seat belongs unto Alexander m'Gruther of Miggor his airs & assignays having paid for building the same as his proportione the sum of ffifteen pounds thirteen shillings and four pennies scots money." etc.

The prominence of the McGrouthers in the district is clearly shown by the position of their seat in the gallery, immediately above the pulpit and in the most conspicuous place. Further, that they are called "of Miggor" is strong proof that they were landowners, as distinct from tenants who would be shown as, for example, "Malcolm McNeiving in Gualnacarrie."

In 1715, Alexander McGrouther followed his master, the Duke of Perth in the Rising of that year and was taken prisoner, along with his brother William, at Preston, in November of that year. In the company of other prisoners, they were marched to London and were ordered to trial. However, mercy prevailed, and Alexander was released under the Act of Indemnity of 1717 and returned to Scotland.

In 1745, Alexander again girded on his weapons, and with his son, also Alexander, was taken prisoner at Carlisle. They would be among those parishioners on whose behalf, the Rev. Mr Menzies of Comrie rode all the way to Carlisle to plead their cause with the Duke of Cumberland. His pleading was in vain and the prisoners were taken to London. Here, the younger Alexander died in gaol in 1746, before he could be tried. The father, now a man in his seventies, was confined in hideous conditions, and eventually sentenced to deportation. The state of his health prolonged the date of his departure, and as the years moved, his case was taken up by many notables in London. He was finally released at the end of 1749 and returned home. He died probably at Craigneich, in 1752.

The story of the McGrouthers of Glenartney gives a strong indication of the powers of the great landowners in the Highlands of Scotland, before the abolition of heritable jurisdictions after the '45. The clan system, though paternalistic in origin and conception, did, indeed, so far as the lower orders were concerned, give rise to many hardships. The Drummonds are not a clan—they are a family with immense territorial possessions and with many adherents among the gentry in these lands, and with a large following of small folk, the farmers, crofters and cottars. The family-oriented Highland Scots gave almost unswerving loyalty to such as they considered the head of the family, who might not even be of their own name. What might have been the future for such as the McGrouthers had they refused to fight, if the Stuarts had been successful in their bid for the crown? There is evidence from the trial of Alexander that he was under duress, in that "the Duke of Perth, whose vassal he was, had forced him into the rebellion, threatening, if he did not immediately join the army, to burn all his houses, destroy his lands and drive his cattle away."

It is fortunate for Scotland, and the Highlands in particular, that the feudal powers of the chiefs and great landowners were broken irrevocably after the '45 and the natural law of Scotland applied to the country as a whole. The minatory terms of Drummond's letter to William McGrouther in 1713, are sufficient to show what a great landowner unquestioningly expected from those who lived within his bounds, be they tenants, crofters, or even owners of the land in their own right.

On the 17th. February 1755 was born Helen McGrouther, to Alexander McGrouther and his wife Helen Forrester. On the death of her father and of her two sisters who shared his estate, she became the sole owner of Meigar. She disposed of the property to Robert Dundas of Melville in 1811, and thus brought to an end the association of her family with Glenartney. In 1829 she erected in Tullichettle graveyard a table stone which still stands, with this almost undecipherable inscription:

Here are deposited the remains of
Alexander McGruther, Esq. of Meigor
who departed this life 28 March 1797
in the eighty second year of his age,
and of
Mrs Helen Forrester his wife who died 28th April 1792,
aged seventy one,
Their daughters.
Elizabeth born 11th Jany, 1753 who died 23rd May 1785
Veronica born 15th June 1759 who died 1st Jan 1808
and Janet born 15th Nov 1762 who died 15th May 1798
are interred with them in this place.
James, David, Duncan, William and John
all died in foreign countries.
Miss Helen McGruther
The sole survivor of the family raised this monument
to their memory
A.D. 1820
Her body now lies below.
She was born 8th Jany. 1755 and died 23rd March 1831.
Much and justly regretted.

The Session Book of Comrie Parish Kirk has the following:

Comrie 26th. Decr. 1805.

Announced by Minr. that Miss Margaret M'Gruther daughter of Dr. Duncan M'Gruther late of Miggor and

F

Drummond Earnoch who was interrred in the family burying place within the Churchyard of Tullichettle on Decr. 22nd. 1801 had bequeathed to the poor of the parish of Tullichettle £10 Stg. which sum, agreeable to her will, had been transmitted to the Minr. upon her mother's death.

And so, after many centuries of habitation in Comrie and Glenartney, the McGrouthers fade into the past. There are none here now.

CHAPTER XIV

EARTHQUAKES

It would be difficult, if not indeed remiss, to speak of Comrie without making reference to its Earthquake notoriety. Such is the history of these phenomena in this area that Comrie has been called "the Home of Earthquakes". The village stands just to the north of the Great Highland Boundary Fault, which runs N.E. to S.W. across Scotland from about Stonehaven to Helensburgh; undoubtedly it is earth movements associated with this Fault which have occasioned the many slight motions and noises, now much more seldom felt and heard, which have given Comrie its reputation. No doubt there were not infrequent shocks and shakes in former years but it was not until the Rev. Samuel Gilfillan, Minister of the Secession Kirk of Comrie, maintained a record of a series of shocks which occurred during his ministry that we learn just how frequently those shocks occurred. The record covers no less than seventy shocks between 1792 and 1814. "The most striking", he says, "was on 24th February 1799, and it is of the Lord's mercies we are not consumed. It happened ten minutes before 2 P.M. I was preaching from Isaiah xlvii, and 4, on the power of Christ our Redeemer, and was arguing from His raising the dead at the Last Day that He has infinite power, when lo! the shock came." He goes on to say that the noise was "awfully loud" and "awfully tremendous", to remark that the church was full, and that "a deep sigh pervaded the congregation." Also interested in the earthquake phenomenon was the Rev. Ralph Taylor who lived at Ochtertyre in 1789. He maintained a record and wrote a report to the Royal Society of Edinburgh, but as his home was just beyond the range of the shocks which were mostly confined to Comrie, only a few shocks were felt as far east as Ochtertyre. Mr. Taylor left the district in 1791 and he was succeeded as "Secretary to the Earthquakes" by Mr. Gilfillan who for a period of thirty years kept a record of the times of the quakes and the phenomena connected with them.

Mr. Gilfillan's records after his death, were fortunately brought to the attention of Mr. David Milne, a man of means, by his son, the Rev. George Gilfillan. There was a renewal of earthquake activity in October 1839 and two local men began keeping careful records, Mr. Peter Macfarlane, postmaster of Comrie, and Mr. James Drummond, a shoemaker in the village. Mr. Macfarlane attended mainly to the shocks while Mr. Drummond concentrated on the earth-sounds. Sadly Mr. Drummond became obsessed with theorising and speculation as to the seat and origin of the Comrie earthquakes and in a disputatious document to the British Association even veered off into the realms of theology. He convinced himself that the quakes had their place of origin in a quarry which had been opened up in the corner of Comrie House park on the banks of the Lednock.

Not only did he maintain his register, Mr. Macfarlane constructed pendulums for detecting earthquakes and tracing their direction. In order to determine the intensity of quakes he drew up one of the earliest seismic scales ever devised. It was a scale containing ten degrees, the highest being that of the intensity of the principal shocks of 23rd October 1839. The scale was known as the Comrie scale. Mr. Macfarlane collaborated with Mr. Milne who encouraged him in his efforts and for some time his records were reported on by Mr. Milne, who was instrumental in obtaining the appointment of a Committee of the British Association "to register the shocks of earthquakes in Scotland and Ireland." The Committee reported from 1839 until 1844 when it was not reappointed as earthquakes became then infrequent in Comrie. The main work of the committee appears to have been the construction of instruments which would record the time and direction of the shocks. It was Mr. Milne who first used the term 'seismometer'.

At the end of 1840, three seismometers were put up in Comrie distirct, an inverted pendulum 10ft.8ins. long, placed in the steeple of Comrie Parish Church; an inverted pendulum of 39 ins. long at Comrie House, and a common pendulum of 39 ins. in Garrichrew, close to Cluan Hill. Next year seven new instruments were set up, namely, four inverted pendulums at Crieff, St. Fillans, Glenlednock and at Kinlochmoidart, near Strontian. Meantime Mr. Macfarlane had built above his home in Dunira Street an observatory which for long dominated the skyline above what is now Brough and Macpherson's shop. Here was provided an instrument consisting of four horizontal tubes slightly turned up at each end and filled with mercury. Finally, two instruments for recording vertical motion, consisting of a horizontal bar fixed to a solid wall by means of a strong flat watchspring and loaded at the free end, were set up, one in Mr. Macfarlane's house and the other at Kinlochmoidart. However the instruments were not sufficiently sensitive for the purpose as they were displaced only twice during the first half of 1841 while in the same period, 27 shocks were distinctly felt in Comrie. Earthquakes reached their highest number in 1844 when 32 were felt in Comrie district and gradually diminished in frequency thereafter so that only 7 were noted between 1849 and 1874. Mr. Macfarlane kept his record until he died in 1874, having felt and recorded more than 300 earthquakes in his lifetime. A slight renewal of activity in 1869 attracted the attention of the Committee who now adopted what was thought might prove a more suitable instrument, that suggested by Mr. Mallet. This was set up in a small stone structure on the Drumearn estate of Mr. Peter Drummond. The building still stands on a rocky outcrop facing the roadway through the Ross. However, as the activity of 1869 was but temporary, the Mallet apparatus never had a practical test. There can be few natives of Comrie who have not several times been aware of the shock of an earthquake. It is quite unmistakable, and has been described sometimes as if a heavy vehicle were passing on the roadway, or like the blow of a heavy fist beneath one's feet. There are no records of structural damage to houses or injuries to persons. Sometimes a slight shaking will cause crockery to rattle, but little else.

There should be no need for newcomers to Comrie to emulate the natives of mid-19th. century who, on a severe shock being felt, betook themselves to the Secession Kirk where they engaged in religious exercises until an early hour, or like the summer visitors who arrived by coach and expressed a strong wish to experience an earthquake, and by chance had their wish granted, much to their alarm which led to a speedy and early departure by the next coach.

The Earthquake House in Drumearn Park. Built in 1869. Primitive apparatus installed here was the very first to record earthquakes anywhere in the world.

CHAPTER XV

AN EXCURSION INTO GLENLEDNOCK

The river Lednock over part of its length forms the eastern boundary of the Parish of Comrie and the Western Edge of the joint Parish of Monzievaird and Strowan. The boundary veers off east of Fintullich and climbs to the heights of Ben Chonzie where it follows the hilltops before descending to the north shore of Loch Earn by the Beich Burn.

The Lednock nowadays is little more than a stream-let since the great Hydro-Electric dam was constructed above Spout Rolla. Those of us who remember it from long ago have vivid memories of the raging torrent it could become in time of high spate. Almost at the junction with the Earn was set up in 1854 the gas-works of which not a trace now remains. The Comrie Gas Light Company was formed by local businessmen and tradesmen who whole-heartedly gave it their finan-cial support. Soon thereafter, many homes in the village were supplied with coal gas for lighting and cooking and the streets illuminated from wrought iron lampposts. The lamps gave off a pale warm glow which fell in a circle around them and these were favourite places for children's play in the evenings. The lights were lit by hand in the gloaming and extingui-shed around ten o'clock. On nights when there was a moon, no lights were lit, even if the moon did not rise before bedtime. Older folk have happy memories of the leeries of our time, Sparkie Crerar and Colin Gillies. Bigger houses around the village such as Auchenross and Aberuchill Castle made their own gas from calcium carbide plants and somewhat later, some like Dunira, Comrie House and the House of Ross, installed early electric power plants driven by water from the Boltachan Burn, Comrie House Dam on the Lednock, and the Mill of Ross Dam on the Earn. The Grampian Electric Supply Company undertook the supply of light and power about 1922.

The present iron bridge over the Lednock together with the Railway bridge and the accommodation bridge leading to Comrie House were typical Caledonian fiddle-bow bridges built about 1895. The latter two bridges have now been demolished and a laminated timber structure in memory of the late Sir Robert Dundas takes their place. A few yards to the east of the bridge is the Scottish Episcopal Church, built in 1884 and dedicated to St. Serf. Almost opposite on the west bank of the stream is the Roman Catholic Church of St. Margaret's converted by the late Rev. Father Williamson of Tomperran, from a row of workers' cottages known, strangely, as the Transvaal.

A little further on, on the east bank, overlooking the Laggan Park playing field and below the Golf Course, is Coneyhill, built on the bailey of a Norman Motte.

The river Lednock about this area was once very much of a "workhorse" from the time of Lord Melville of Dunira who once owned Comrie. He had built a dam over the river above Comrie House which supplied power to a corn mill and a sawmill, and further down a woollen mill which employed many hands and later, even, a distillery. These are all gone now and even the name of the roadway leading to them, once named Mill Lane has been changed to Nurse's Lane. What is now called Drummond Street was once Lednick or Lednaig Street.

As stated in another chapter, the traveller from the Toll of Comrie, or modern Melville Square, went northwards through The Acres or Acreland fronting Comrie House. Until fairly recently this way passed through The Tunnel which once carried the Caley Railway to St. Fillans. Close by the tunnel stood the miniature Rifle Range much frequented in the years after the First World War when old soldiers renewed memories of bygone service and kept their eye in against future trouble. Not a few Comrie laddies were initiated here into the use of the Small Bore Rifle under the watchful eye of Peter Peddie and Willie Anton. The acrid smell of cordite readily comes back from that tiny shed. The Boy Scouts' hut, a disused wooden Army hut from the War, was the early meeting place of the 21st. Perthshire. If memory serves, the hut was taken down and re-erected as the Annexe to the Public Hall.

The acres were divided up into small allotments which supplied the needs of the villagers in the surrounding streets, for many of them kept a cow in the early 19th. century. These cows were under the charge of a herd-laddie, whose job it was to pass up the street and collect the animals as he passed to the grazings in the Coo Park off Monument Road or to the Balloch Park of the present Lechkin Farm. In the late afternoon, the cows were brought home, and as they passed along they would drop off, each at its own entry or pend. On the north side of Drummond Street are several lanes leading to the Acres or to Back o' Toon Lane, Nurse's Lane, Pudding Lane, Feuars' Lane, Melville Lane, and in Dundas Street, there are three covered pends and, leading to the Earn, the lane by the Old School and Bowlie Lane. These gave access to the Earn for drawing of water and for watering of animals.

The street names of Comrie are an indication of its history and the people who were its superiors. Drummond Street is, of course, from the great Drummond family who once held sway over most of Upper Strathearn and much else, Dundas and Dunira lead back, either to Henry Dundas, Viscount Melville or to the Dundases of Beechwood who succeeded him. Burrell is from the Hon. Peter Burrell who married the heiress to the Drummond Estates after their restoration to the family in 1784 following upon their annexation to the Crown after the abortive Rising of 1745.

We leave Comrie by Monument Road, passing on the right, the old Coo Park, just mentioned. Here once stood a long low cottage by the name of Slochd More. A wild rose tree from its garden still flourishes beside the drainage ditch. On the right are the entrance gates to Comrie House, and beyond the park, the once handsomely pillared entrance to Comrie House woods. This footpath or roadway was granted to the folk of Comrie when the Comrie House folk wished to close the old roadway through The Acres as it passed just in front of the mansion. Comrie's association with the Dundases has always been of a most cordial and friendly nature and access to the woods has never been denied. Sadly, the years and the tempests have not been kind to the trees, and the remaining beeches are merely a representation of those which were here even sixty years ago. All the great larches, too, have gone and much poor scrub remains.

Let us keep to the highway. On the left rises up the long ridge of Craig o'Ross to its summit in the Craig itself, known to natives as Turleum top for it is quite bare rock, and to John Brown, teacher in St. Fillans about 1820, as Toptillian. On the summit is the clear impression of the Deil's Footprint which no child, now of mature years, would dream of placing his foot within. If it were not for the screen of poor quality timber here, a superb view could be had to the west to the hills of Aberuchill. Within living memory the Craig wood was clothed in soft timber trees which were cut down during the First World War and never replanted. The trees were followed by a tremendous growth of broom, from end to end, which eventually grew old and, one very hot summer, caught fire and blazed from end to end. One has vivid memories of stirring up the embers as children and being chased by old Hughie Ferguson from Tullibannocher Smiddy who had been put in charge to stop such miscreants as we were.

The divide between the Craig Wood and the other side known as Willie Bain's wood is the Sheugh o' the Balloch. Through here once passed the old roadway to St. Fillans before Lord Melville created the new road at the beginning of the 19th. century. The word Balloch, of course, refers, not to the brae as is often thought, but to the pass through which the old road passed. And who was Willie Bain? Nobody now knows but the tradition is that poor Willie long ago hanged himself here on a tree. Above the Sheugh is another hollow, called Willie Bain's Pond. This is partly natural and partly artificial and was, doubtless, a retting pond for the rotting of flax fibres. Impending above the pond is a very notable travelled or errant boulder, grounded here thousands of years ago, as an ice sheet moved down into the strath. There is another similar example on a rocky outcrop above the Glasdale Road just west of the entrance to Lower Lechkin farm, in Twenty Shilling Wood.

Immediately above the Balloch Brae is a small field named the Baker's Park. It is so named as at one time it was rented from Dunira Estate by the local baker who pastured his delivery horse here. The old roadway leading off eastwards from the top of the brae leads to an old quarry in the wood which is named Cracken wood, probably a corruption of Craggan Wood as the woodland is upon a craggy outcrop. The field enclosed by the old roadway and Comrie House Wood is named simply, Balloch Park. This park was once part of the common grazing land of the cottars of the west end of Comrie.

The farm of Lechkin, once named Torry Farm, has been farmed by several generations of the Mitchell family. The original John Mitchell came here about 1872 and has been followed by his son, grandson and great grandson. The farm land is now greatly augmented by lands in the Ross, at Chattan and near Comrie House.

The original farmhouse still stands and is an example of an 18th. century long-house, as the living accommodation is continuous with a small byre in which calves or stirks could be kept. It is a tradition in the family that when John Mitchell came here he found tied to a rafter in this small byre, a handful of rowan twigs, put there to keep away the witches. The spring which enabled the house and steading to be built here flows at the roadside. It has been known to run dry only four times in the past seventy odd years. The field below the farmhouse is the Whinny Park for obvious reasons. At its foot runs a small stream flowing from a small marshy area between the Twenty Pence Wood and Pollyrigg Wood. Here it was once possible to guddle a good Yellow Trout, or even a small seatrout. Beyond the stackyard is a small field known as Saut and Barley's. The reason for the name is because this was owned once by an old mason named James Carmichael whose nickname was Saut and Barley. From the stackyard area, below the highway runs an old roadway which traverses the foot of Pollyrigg wood and continues on through the fields of Tullybannocher East and onwards to Drumna Cille and Loch Boltachan.

The field above the roadway on the right is the Quarry park, named from the great whinstone quarry from which came the stone to build the Free Kirk of Comrie and many homes in the village. To the east lies the field named The Level, which is the only nearly level field on the farm and the Atween the Woods field. Above the Quarry is Pollyrigg field and higher still, the strangely named Drumachople. This name is a corruption of Druim a Capull or Ridge of the Mare. The sharp rise and bend of the roadway beyond is called Balnasackit, from Baile an t-Sagairt, place of the priest. The roadway here is lined by ancient and now much decayed Spanish Chestnut trees relics of the days when this land belonged to the Drummond Estates. The Drummond family of Perth were greatly in favour of such chestnut trees to embellish their domains and they are found in many places throughout the strath.

It must have been a hazardous job to construct the roadway along the Lednock, above the Cauldron gorge and below Dunmore Hill. Both sides of the roadway have great stands of oak coppice, again relics of the days when oak coppicing and oak barking were of great value to the landlords.

Many years ago there was a proposal to throw a light bridge across the Cauldron but nothing came of it. Certainly a bridge here would have afforded a superb position from which to view the gorge and cascade. The Deil's Cauldron is in Gaelic, Slochd an Donais, the Devil's Pit, and it is said that in ancient days there dwelt here a Water Sprite who laid traps for the unwary and held frequent converse when the water was in spate with his brother Sprite who had his home in Spout Rolla, further up the glen.

On emerging from the gorge one finds a complete change of scene. The road for the next two miles or so runs almost level with many twists and bends, with short dips and braes. The view is extensive with Carn Hois and Ben Chonzie rising majestically on the right and in the farther west the heights of Craiguch-dach. In the nearer distance descend the Cushavachan Rocks, a series of great outcrops with descriptive Gaelic names. The Eagle's Crag, the Black Crag, the Grey Crag, the Raven's Crag and the Cross or Transverse Crag. The field on the right is the Castle Park, so named from the slight eminence close by the Shaky Brig which we have been told is actually a Motte from mediaeval times. It surely is a distinctive feature with its now disappearing circular wall and its 'hedge' of alternate oak and chestnut trees. The Shaky Brig, now recently rebuilt, probably figures more strongly than any other feature, in the minds of Comrie folk. It gives foot access to the farms of Balmuick to the east and to Carroglen and Lurg to the northwards. Immediately alongside the bridge is the old ford which carried the early roadway into the glen by the Eight

Merkland of Kingarth.

On the left rise the craggy Craw Rocks, for centuries the home of Jackdaws, whose eggs in less enlightened times were plundered by boys at some risk to life and limb. Curving round the base of the rocks is the Maam Road which climbs to the saddle between Dunmore Hill and the Crappich Hills of Dunira. The views from the summit up and down Strathearn are superb, while from the Monument one has almost an aerial view of the village of Comrie and Strathearn as far east as the Lomonds of Fife and west to the mighty Grampian outliers, Ben More and Stobinian, Ben Vorlich, Stuc a Chroin, Dundurn and Ben Halton. There are few finer or greater prospects of Scotland.

Near the Maam Road, below the Craw Rocks, flows out the spring of clear, cold water, known as the Kinkhoast Well. Kinkhoast is Lowland Scots for Whooping Cough and it was once thought that to drink of the water would prove a sovereign remedy for the malady.

To the right of the roadway lies the farm and farmhouse of Kingarth and mouldering below the turf and lost among the bracken is the old farmtoun of Glaslarich. Close inspection reveals the foundations of many homes, dykes and limekilns which were the abodes of crofters before the days of the Clearances. Over the ridge behind Kingarth lie the small ruined remains of Tynacroy and Balmenoch. The walls of the former still remain to a height of about five feet and the site of the garden, barn and millgang show clearly. The place was still being farmed as a unit until about 1850. Half a mile further west is Tynasithe with the remains of two homes, one of the 19th. century and an earlier one, a long house, probably from at least a century before. On a knowe stands a superb kiln for drying corn or burning limestone. Near these places are several aged and decaying ash trees whose timbers were used for forming the primitive farm tools, and some aged larch trees whose timbers were used to form the roof trees and rafters of the early homes. Nearby, too, are the sure proof of ancient settlement, beds of nettles, the leaves of which were used in making soups in times of hardship, which must have been frequent.

One half mile further and we come to The Drum, not a noticeable feature but of considerable notoriety in times of snow storms, as the action of the wind builds here great snowdrifts which, even today, can take several days to cut through with modern machinery. Not so many years ago, only pairs of hands and shovels were employed and during the war even gangs of German prisoners spent days here. Below the Drum the ancient road to Tynasithe and Tynacroy bears off to the right and ahead lies the old bridge, Anaba Brig named from the Ford of the Cows, Ath na Ba.

There is a fascinating tradition regarding the field lying to the west of the bridge and to the left of the road. By nature one would believe it should be part of Ballindalloch Farm, part of Dunira Estate. It is, in fact, part of Invergeldie Estate. The story is that the two lairds once played a game of cards, the stake being this field, and the Laird of Dunira lost.

Straight ahead is Fintullich and the old trackway leading off to the north bank of the Lednock at the base of the hills to Lurg and Carroglen. In droving times this was the route followed by the herds coming from Lochtayside. They proceeded thence by Balmuick, through what is now the west edge of Comrie Golf Course, and so to Crieff. At Fintullich once stood the primitive, heather thatched school and schoolhouse, supported by the efforts of the S.S.P.C.K. The later school, was the quaint, conical-roofed, square edifice at the highest point of the road beyond Fintullich. It must have been a chilly spot as it is completely exposed to all the winds which blow. Its life probably was about a century until in the 1920's a fine new school and schoolhouse were built a little farther on, in a site more protected from the elements. A public meeting held at the time in Comrie raised strong objections to the expense involved, one irate ratepayer

Tynashee in Glenlednock. Ruins of 19th century barn and ruins of a long house of 18th or 17th century structure. Hills of Ballindalloch and Castle Castle Rocks in background. Far right on rock outcrop stands 19th century school. Fintallich in right distance is site of S.S.P.C.K. school built in 1713.

asking, indignantly, "What wad a teacher be wantin' wi' two parlours?" All glen pupils are now driven to school in Comrie or Crieff. The pleasant small villa sheltering behind the pinewood on the knowe was once the schoolmistress's house.

The farm road to East and West Ballindalloch leads off to the left behind the copse and to Balnacoul. East Ballindalloch was tenanted for generations by a family of Campbells, while for some three hundred years Balnacoul was in the possession of McGregors, who produced over the years not a few unruly characters. One, long-searched for by the authorities, ventured to the Tryst of Crieff, was recognised, and while attempting to escape, was shot and killed by the dragoons in attendance at the Tryst. Others, at an earlier time, were implicated in the dastardly murder in Glenartney Forest of Drummond of Drummondernoch.

Immediately behind Balnacoul rears up the scree and boulder strewn slopes of Balnacoul Castle. One looks in vain for sign of a castle as it is merely the towering pinnacles and rocky spires which have given the hill its name.

Shortly after passing the "New School", we see the Shepherds' cottages of Cushavachan, and cross the sparkling Geldie Burn, to Invergeldie, proper, with its shooting lodge, farmhouse and workers' homes. An ancient drove road takes off here to skirt the western foot of Ben Chonzie, and leads to Ardtalnaig on the south shore of Loch Tay and to Upper Glenalmond. It was used by the cattle drovers and in later years, after the coming of sheep, by great flocks of sheep coming down to the Lowlands for sale and wintering, to be transported, before the days of road transport, in the sheep-trains of the Caledonian Railway, often one hundred trucks in length, which in the autumn passed, almost nose to tail for about a week. Their passing was quite an event of the year. Sadly, one year, by some mischance, such a train was derailed at St. Fillans station with immense slaughter of animals, butchers from miles around being mustered to end their sufferings.

Leaving Innergeldie, we shortly come in sight of Spout Rolla. At the foot of the climb the old road into Glenmaik takes off to the left. This is a bonnie, wee glen with a derelict cottage and the mouldering remains of many small homes with a neat walled garden in which no crops have grown these hundred years or more. The old track leads to the peatworkings of Monevie, whence many of the older homes in Comrie dug their winter supplies, and which still figure in their title deeds. The Hydro road leads over the divide into sight of Loch Lednock, created by the great, but-tressed dam thrown across the river above the Spout, which only comes alive again when the waters spill over the top of the dam. This seldom happens now, as water means money to the Hydro Board. Sunk beneath the waters and seen only in times of drought are the old shepherds' cottages of Bovain at the east end of the loch, and at the west end, of Bowalker (Bouachdair), while on the south shore lies Keplandie. The road is now merely a pathway but was once a drove road coming from Ardeonaig on Loch Tay.

At various places up the glen one comes on the re-mains of shielings, the summer homes of the women and children who tended the cows on the summer grass and converted the milk into butter and cheese. Higher still around are the remains of attempts at mining such minerals as lead and copper. These were largely the work of the Marquisses of Breadalbane, but they did not find much success.

CHAPTER XVI

TALES OF COMRIE AND ITS FOLK

Many stories of Comrie and district have been recorded in books and newspaper articles which are now long out of print. If these tales are not re-recorded, they will merge into oblivion. As they throw valuable light on the days and ways of the past, which go to make the real history of this place, they still have a value and interest for later generations. So, for Auld Lang Syne, here are some of these stories which may not be generally known.

The following two stories concern members of a family who lived at the Mill at Milton. Peter Cram was the miller who was dispossessed about 1815 by his landlord, the Laird of Lawers. After a short period in Comrie working as weavers, Peter and his wife Janet Key, uprooted their family and emigrated to Upper Canada in 1820.

ADVENTURE WITH A BOAR

It was customary before the days of compulsory education for boys and girls to have their school days interrupted so that they could help out the family finances in planting and gathering crops, in barking the oak for the production of tannery materials, in herding cattle, in bird–scaring on newly sown grain, and in many other occupations. In the early days of the Agricultural Revolution, their many pairs of hands were invaluable. Often they were taken away to full-time work at the tender age of eight or nine.

One such child in Comrie was George Ferguson who was fee'd to Tam Galloway, tenant at the Carse of Strowan. Geordie soon became a great favourite with his master and all about the farm. There being few hedges or dikes or fences, the animals roamed around the farm much as they pleased during the daytime, and it was Geordie's job as the herd-laddie to keep them from trespassing among the corn or other growing crops. A large boar lived on the farm and he allowed Geordie to ride astride him and he would carry him wherever he was directed to go. In the evenings, Geordie was sometimes sent to Comrie for messages, and thither the boar would carry him until they arrived near the village, when the boar was dismissed to return to the Carse on his own.

No matter how late Geordie might be in returning home, the boar was certain to be home in good order. However, on one occasion, while returning alone, the boar decided to vary his travels and turned off the turnpike road at the Milton, and found his way into the mill. Work had been stopped for the night, but the door had not been properly fastened and the boar lay down in the warmth beside the drying kiln. Finding his quarters warm and comfortable, the boar lay quietly beneath the kiln fire, and slept soundly.

Early next morning, old Peter Cram rose early, and taking his cruizie in his hand went to the kiln to replenish the fire or relight it if it had gone out. The morning was pitch dark, and he was scantily clothed, as he intended to go back to bed for a while. The fire was very low, and he took some seeds and some damp straw and put them on the fire. This created a great smoke, which partially blinded him as he hunkered before the fire. The boar woke up with a terrific grunt and made a rush for the door. Catching the miller between his legs it carried him outside on its back with his face to its tail. Outside, Peter fell off, and making a bolt for the house, he told his wife that something uncanny had tried to carry him away, and that he would not leave the house until daylight came in, whatever might happen to the grain drying on the kiln.

For some time the cause of Peter's fright was a mystery, but when Geordie Ferguson heard the story, he suspected that the boar had something to do with it.

The following story was brought back long ago from Beckwith, now Carleton Place in Ontario, where many Comrie emigrants first took up lands in what was then, Upper Canada, among them the Cram family from Milton.

John or Jock Cram was the first of his family to leave Comrie. Along with over 30 grown-up young men belonging to the Seceder congregation he sailed in the summer of 1818. No doubt, it was the glowing reports of his new land which he sent back home that decided the rest of the family to follow.

Jock was the happy-go-lucky sort, and as he found plenty of work available, he soon got on well. A great number of Scots folk had settled where Jock was located and he soon became a great favourite among them. There were also a good many Irish in the district. The Scots did not care much for them as they were rather free in their drinking of poteen and indulged in much uproar amongst themselves which made them uncomfortable neighbours to the Scots. However, Jock became as friendly with the Irish as he was with the Scots, and at last became enamoured of an Irish lass, and after a time they were married.

They lived happily for a time, but at last Jock's wife decided he was rather too slow for her and they finally resolved to separate. One day the wife's friends came with a wagon, loaded it with her effects and drove away with the wife aboard. After a while on the road, Jock came after them calling to them to stop. They thought he had come to make proposals for his wife's return, but all that Jock had to say was that his wife had left behind one of her wearing gowns and he had brought it with him as he did not want his wife to leave any of her belongings with him.

At a later date the Scots settlers resolved to have a new cemetery in their district. When the Irish heard of this they wanted to have a share of it, but to this proposal a good many of the Scots were much opposed, while others were quite indifferent. Several meetings were held and the matter discussed. At one of the meetings the chairman rose and said that nearly all had voiced their opinions but that Mr. Cram had taken no part at all. Jock then got up and said --"We a' ken that the Irish are a troublesome lot an' no easy to put up wi' at times, but I think if I had six feet o' earth on the tap o' them, I could manage them."

This speech of Jock settled the matter and it was agreed to let the Irish have a share of the cemetery to bury their dead; but whether Jock buried his own wife there we are unable to tell.

To this day the cemetery is known as the Cram Cemetery and old Peter Cram and many of his descendants are buried there, as the stones bear witness.

ILLICIT DISTILLATION OR 'SMUGGLING'

The usual alcoholic drink of Scotsmen until well into the 18th. Century had been ale or claret, the latter for the wealthier classes and imported from Bordeaux. About the middle of the 18th. Century, the drinking of Whisky became more popular, even stern ministers of the Kirk were not averse to a dram. The manufacture of the spirits was almost of the nature of a cottage industry and much was produced in the crofts and in the glens. Indeed, many small farmers would have been hard put to it to meet their landlords' demands for rent, if their otherwise small incomes had not been augmented by the sale of spirits in the local villages and in the towns of the Lowlands. The produce of the "ewie wi' the crookit horn" was in great demand.

Cheating the Revenue was, like poaching, treated as more of a pastime than an offence by most of the folks of those days, and many were the stratagems resorted to to defeat the gaugers and the dragoons; very frequently the latter forces had to be called in aid of the civil powers.

A well-known smuggler in his day was Archie M'Niven who worked as a mason and who lived in Glenartney or, perhaps Blairnroar. You can see several M'Niven stones in Tullichettle graveyard. Archie was one of his own best customers and was often in trouble, but was never caught. He emigrated to Upper Canada in 1829 along with his brother William and the latter's wife and family. Sadly, William died within six weeks of landing and his widow had the daunting task of bringing up six small children in the forest wilderness around Rice Lake, Ontario. Sandy aided her greatly, though he did not change his habits, until one day, he saw the light, and became a reformed character. He wrote two pieces of verse, of the "before and after" kind. These he must have brought back to Comrie on a visit to friends here.

In his Comrie days he narrowly escaped capture on one occasion and had, perforce to secrete his hoard in a kirkyard vault. (One would like to know where, exactly). A considerable part of the smuggled stuff was disposed of in the district, but there was also a band of illicit traders called the Stirling Band, who visited this and other parts of the country, and bought all that they could readily obtain. They were a fearless lot and were well mounted. The excisemen had to be well prepared before they encountered the Stirling Band.

One of the most noted smugglers in our district was Peter M'Arthur who resided on a small croft on Aberuchill estate high up near Montillie. A field here is still named 'McArthur Park' and a few of the stones of his house yet remain. The location of his croft allowed him a wide view of the country and any approach to it was difficult. A married man with a family, he indulged to a large extent in producing illicit spirits to augment his income. The Excisemen were well aware of this, and several raids were made on his premises.

On one occasion a party of gaugers was almost at the house before they were observed, and as a quantity of illicit stuff was in the house at the time, Peter and his family were in a sad fix. Peter's brother, Arthur, was in the house at the time. Glancing around he spotted an empty kirn. Seizing it, he got it on his shoulder, dashed from the house and made for the hills at the back. The Excisemen at once gave chase, and, Arthur being young and athletic, led them a fine dance. While the chase was proceeding, Peter and his family busied themselves in getting the house in order, and when the party returned having captured Arthur and the empty kirn, there was no evidence to find. The officers knew they had been done, but there was no more that they could do.

But Peter did not always fare so well. On another occasion he was caught red-handed and taken prisoner by a mounted party, who were conveying him along the road from Aberuchill to Comrie. When passing the Ross Wood, a little to the west of the Mill of Ross, Peter complained that they were going too fast, and that he could not keep up with them. The leader of the party ordered one of his men to pull up to the side of the dike, and Peter was ordered to mount behind the horseman. Peter at once got on top of the dike, and leaping into the wood, he bade them goodbye. The party unslung their carbines and called on him to surrender, but Peter took his way through the thick wood, and when the coast was clear, found his way home.

Peter was taken on another occasion and was conveyed

as far as Crieff, on his way to Perth for trial. The escort halted for refreshments at a house at the west end of the town, and, while they were being served, Peter saw his opportunity and made a bolt for the street, which he safely reached. He ran down Tannery Street. The door of the tannery was open and he rushed through and got out of the back door. Making his way to the Earn near where it joins the Turret, he plunged in and got safely over to the other side. The river was in spate and none of his pursuers risked swimming over, and Peter got safely away.

Ultimately, Peter's luck ran out and he served a spell in prison. He lived to a good old age and was greatly liked by his neighbours as he was of an obliging and kind disposition.

On another occasion a company of dragoons, who were stationed in Auchterarder, rode into Comrie accompanied by several Excise officers. The villagers immediately suspected that some trouble was afoot and those in the know let it be known that a party with a quantity of smuggled spirits was about due from the Breadalbane country, and that by that time they should be in Glenlednock.

A number of young weavers at once left their looms and, taking the road leading past Comrie House, they met Donald Garrow, a noted smuggler with two small casks over his shoulders. They informed him how matters stood in Comrie, but he thought that they were merely trying to frighten him. However, when he saw they were in earnest, he told them that the main body was coming along behind.

The young lads hurried along and met the main party almost opposite Kingarth Farmhouse. At that time there were several clumps of trees growing near, and there were several hollows in the ground. The smugglers had two light carts with them, and these with the horses were taken into one of the hollows and concealed. The lads returned homewards and met the Excise party coming up near the Deil's Cauldron.

The dragoons amused themselves by striking the boys with the flat of their swords, and the lads got away into the wood. They waited until they saw the party ride up the glen past the smugglers' hiding place. When the coast was clear, the weavers returned and assisted the smugglers to bring their wares to Comrie, where they were taken into Elder Ferguson's public-house. (The Elder's house was 40 yards east of the present Melville Square in Drummond Street). When the searchers returned to Comrie, they were much chagrinned to see the smugglers and the Comrie lads hob-nobbing together, and evidently having a good joke at their expense. A vigorous search was begun, and when the trail was becoming too hot, the whisky was taken from the Elder's house and carried across the lane at the back and up into the garret of the Rev. Samuel Gilfillan's manse, which was but a few yards from the Elder's house.

The manse is attached to the church, and there was a small opening between the garret and the church, where, when her children were young, Mrs. Gilfillan used to sit and hear her husband preach while she was nursing her bairns. The smuggled stuff was removed through this opening into the church and put into a kind of press beneath the pulpit, and there it remained for some time until the search was abandoned, Mr. Gilfillan preaching over the top of it Sabbath after Sabbath for a time.

THE HUNTING OF THE WHITE HIND

The Forest of Glenartney has since Stewart times been the scene of many hunting episodes in the lives of our kings, and of at least one queen. James III and James IV hunted here, as did Mary, Queen of Scots and Darnley. Surely one of the more bizarre episodes is that of the Hunting of the White Hind of Corrie Ba. Corrie Ba is in the wildest part of Perthshire on the borders of Argyll, south of Glencoe, the Black Mount. While hunting here, the Earl of Mar sighted a white hind, whose presence he reported to his sovereign, James VI and I. This happened in 1621 when James had long been absent from Scotland, enjoying the enlarged court life of London. James was very keen that this rare animal be captured and in 1622 instructed one, John Scandaver, a noted hunter in the gentle Home Counties, to take with him two assistants and travel to Scotland to capture the white hind. James with his foolish, bright mind, was so fired with enthusiasm that, though he personally knew the hazards of the Scottish hills, he failed to consider that John Scandaver had merely shown his prowess in the deer parks of southern England, and was ill-equipped, therefore, to undertake such difficulties and hardships as he would certainly encounter. Having spent his working life among the pleasant woodlands and gentle hills of his homeland, Scandaver had no conception of the heatherclad mountains, steep hillsides and dangerous swollen rivers. The poor man must have had many second thoughts and misgivings as he trailed day after day over the moors and black peat bogs of Rannoch Moor. Failing in his enterprise, he was persuaded by Mar to make a second try the next year and in the meantime to travel to the Royal Forest of Glenartney, and to try there to capture live deer. He seems to have been well received in Glenartney and well entertained but it appears that his second enterprise was no more successful and the same year he returned to London, to lick his wounds, not the first Englishman who failed to take Scotland into account.

THE ROADMENDER AND THE RECTOR

One sunny afternoon, the newly-appointed Rector of the Episcopal Kirk, which had been but recently built near the foot of the Lednock, was taking his

Robbie the Stane Breaker (Knapper). Note three thumbs.

walk through Comrie House woods to view the Deil's Cauldron. Duly impressed, he scrambled upwards to the public roadway leading to Upper Glenlednock. It happened that Robbie Napier, the stonebreaker, was sitting on a pile of rough road metal, tapping away with his knapping hammer. Thinking to have a little fun at the expense of the simple Countryman, the Rector approached Robbie and jocularly remarked, "Surely, you don't really believe that the 'Old Gentleman' lives down in the Cauldron?" "Na, na," replied Robbie, staunch Presbyterian as he was, "He's no' there noo. Sin they pit up that wee widden erection at the fit o' the Lednock, he's ta'en up his abode doon there."

THE SUFFRAGETTES

One afternoon in February 1914 two well dressed, well-spoken ladies called at the door of Mrs. Andrew McDonald who then lived at Rossbank, The Ross. They asked for directions to the House of Ross, and were told that the family was not in residence as they customarily passed the winter season in their home in Edinburgh. That night the House of Ross which had been built as recently as 1908 by Mrs. McLagan was burned to the ground with most of its contents. Local villagers did what they could to salvage furnishings but the efforts of the primitive fire brigade proved unavailing. The same night Aberuchill castle was set alight, when only two of the maids were at home. Luckily, the maids, who slept high up in the building, were awakened by the smell of smoke and with the hard work of the estate fire brigade managed to contain the damage. As if this were not enough, a large private house, Allt an Fionn in St. Fillans, was put to the flames and destroyed. Mercifully, there was no loss of life at any of the fires and it may well be that the suffragettes, who were blamed for the occurrences, were aware that the families would be in winter quarters elsewhere, and the presence of the maids in the castle was not known to them. Thus was Comrie brought violently into the forefront of the struggle for votes for women.

A MARTYR FOR FREEDOM

In 1817, Alexander McLaren, who hailed from Aberuchill, was tried for sedition. He was employed as a weaver in Kilmarnock, having been trained in the work at Perth and Glasgow. It was stated in evidence that he was a skilled worker who was able to earn more than the majority of his fellow-workers at the same trade, and that by working 15 hours a day he was able to earn five shillings a week. The charge of sedition arose out of a speech he had made at a public meeting held to protest against high taxation and to petition for parliamentary reform. He proposed that a petition should be presented to the king setting forth the grievances of his subjects in the matter of high taxation, and the belief that too much revenue was being squandered in pensions and sinecures for Government hangers-on. He affirmed the petitioners' loyalty and allegiance to the king, with suitable compliments to His Majesty, but was then alleged to have said that if the king would not listen to their complaints "then to Hell with our allegiance." He was convicted and sentenced to six months imprisonment in the Tolbooth Jail in Edinburgh, and to give caution for three years good behaviour in the sum of £40 sterling. On his release he was presented with a silver snuff-box engraved, "A token of respect presented by the Friends of the Parliamentary Reform in Kilmarnock to Alexander McLaren on his liberation from the Canongate Jail, October 7th, 1817, after having been confined six months for nobly standing forth in the glorious cause of Freedom." *(The beautiful snuff-box is in the possession of Mr. Sandy Stewart, Laird of Ardvorlich, whose father, the late Major Jock Stewart allowed me to hold it in my hands. Alexander McLaren was one of their ancestors).*

COMRIE AND ALASKA

Comrie has an indirect connection with far-away Alaska. The Comrie Hotel, known in our youth as Melville House, was run by the Misses Stirling, one of whom had married a Hudson's Bay Chief Factor, Robert Campbell, born at Dalchiorlich in Glenlyon. He rose to be one of the chief officers of the company. In 1840, as factor, he was sent by Governor Simpson to explore the Yukon. He there founded Fort Selkirk and Mount Campbell, one of the highest Yukon peaks is named after him. One of today's modern highways is called, also, the Robert Campbell Highway. The little party of which he was chief discovered the Yukon Valley, and penetrated under great difficulties into Alaska, then Russian territory, with an undefined boundary between it and British territory. If first discovery counted in the settlement of the boundary, the whole of the Klondyke hinter-land should belong to Canada, because no white man's foot had ever traversed these regions before Robert Campbell led his party over them.

When the Louis Riel Rebellion broke out in Canada, Campbell was in charge of Fort Garry, where Winnipeg now stands, but he was away on his annual trading trip. Some years before, he had married Miss Stirling and she and their children were left behind in the fort, which was in charge of Thomas Scott, and could not be held against the rebels within and without. Mrs. Campbell rallied together some fugitives and faithful Indians, who seized upon boats, and with them escaped, while "President" Riel and his half-breeds looted the fort and murdered Scott. The Riel Rebellion was suppressed in 1870.

There is a letter written by Robert Campbell in 1890 to John McNaughton, Balmeanach, Glen Lyon, in which he mentions, "I have been lately down to Winnipeg seeing my sister-in-law, Miss M.E. Stirling off for Comrie, Scotland, as the winter weather here is too severe for her." Robert Campbell was nicknamed "Manitoba".

CLAW POSTS

It is said that the Duke of Argyll set up at intervals on his hill pastures a series of posts on which his small black cattle could scratch their heads and backs to rid themselves of ticks and other pests. It is said too, that the Highland herdsmen availed themselves of the facility and in doing so would send up a thankful word to the Almighty, "Gott pless the Duke of Argyll, for a claw post every mile."

Early travellers in the Highlands were much disgusted at the sight of the natives scratching and clawing at themselves, as they suffered from some form of itch. The malady was so common that the name of the "Scotch fiddle" was used as a euphemism. It is probable that the cause of this itch was the deplorable living and housing conditions of the poor. Some of their hovels have been described as little better than holes in the ground. They have been described as hardly fit for animals, let alone human beings to live in and, indeed, such was the case, as the animals shared the other, with only a hallan of light wickerwork as separation. The smoke from the fireplace set in the middle of the floor, having no chimney by which to escape, would wreathe around the rafters and eventually find its way out by the doorway or by the window spaces which had no glass, often being stuffed with straw to keep out the cold. The smoke-blackened rafters served as night roosts for the poultry and in wet weather the roof sods would let in the rain to fall in streams on the inmates. In dry weather, earth and worms would drop out of the sods and fall into the cooking utensils. It is no wonder that the poor folks suffered from rheumatism, sore eyes and the itch.

THE FLAMBEAUX

As midnight strikes on Hogmanay in Comrie a strange, time-honoured ceremony takes place—the lighting of the Flambeaux, to herald in the New Year. It is a ceremony that goes back far beyond the memory of folk and when questioned as to its origin, they say, "There have aye been flambeaux, in my father's time and my grandfather's."

The flambeaux are great tall torches, some ten feet in length, swathed for about two feet on top. The poles used are usually smallish birch trees which are cut around October. The swathing is of canvas firmly bound to the shaft with wire, and is subjected to being soaked in a large barrel of paraffin for several weeks.

On Hogmanay night they are brought out and laid against the dyke at the north-east corner of the Auld Kirkyaird, and when the clock strikes are set alight. Some six torches are then seized by the strongest young men and hoisted shoulder-high. Preceded by a piper the procession forms up and the flambeaux are paraded down Drummond Street, back and over Dalginross Bridge and down by Strowan Road to the Square, then along Dunira Street to the Public Hall in Burrell Street and final return to the Square. It takes strong men to complete the circuit, but there are plenty of volunteers to take up the burden.

A motley collection of guisers in varied and fantastic costumes makes the circuit of the village. Prizes are awarded for the more original costumes and a merry time is held around the dying embers of the flambeaux which are set as a bonfire in the Square.

G

The large crowd of followers and onlookers now sets off to first-foot their friends and the village settles back to its quiet ways.

Deil's Cauldron

CHAPTER XVII

COMRIE FOLK ABROAD

I have thought it well to include in the story of Comrie Parish, the following essay on some of the descendants of parishioners whose ancestors, natives of this place, took the long sea-road to Canada many years ago. Experience of meeting many of the Canadians and Americans, and of an extensive correspondence with many others seeking their roots here, has led me to believe that such an essay would not come amiss, and might awaken an interest among those similarly descended, who have remained here. It would have been possible to bring in the names of many more Comrie emigrants, as for years, there has been a steady trickle of enquiries, both by letter and by visitors. It has been an absorbing hobby for myself, and has been of obvious satisfaction to the searchers. Though much has changed since the forebears of these "Scots Abroad" sailed away to begin new lives in new surroundings, enough remains of man's handiwork with which their ancestors were acquainted, to excite the interest of these "cousins" of ours, and nothing more so, than seeing the grave of an ancestor, be it in the Aulk Kirk Yard or at Tullichettle, and even more especially, the mouldering rickle of stones that once were homes, at Tignasithe, Glentarken, Blairnroar and up and down Glenartney.

"Mountains divide us, and the waste of seas--
Yet still the blood is strong, the heart is Highland."

1829--9th. May. -- Nearly sixty families are about to emigrate from the Parish of Comrie to Canada, causing a reduction of from two to three hundred on the amount of its population.--Courant.

This short statement in the newspaper of the day gives some indication of the bloodletting to which Scotland in general, and the Parish of Comrie in particular, was subjected in the later decades of the 18th. and early decades of the 19th. centuries. By some, these movements of people are laid at the door of the Agricultural Revolution, by some are labelled as Improvements, by others, still, as The Clearances. By whatever name, they certainly improved the lot of the Lords and the Lairds, but imposed terrible hardship and heartbreak on the poor folk and the clansmen. One would not argue but that life was hard and often miserable for the dwellers in the hills and glens--but they had known no other, and in our own and neighbouring parishes, from such records and information as we have, were simple, hardworking and God-fearing men and women. Less than a century before they had "come out" in the '45 in support of their lairds and chieftains, and after Culloden, almost literally, found themselves thrown to the wolves.

Certainly, in this district, there is no evidence of the atrocious behaviour of too many landlords and more particularly, their factors. None the less, the throwing of so many small holdings and group farms into larger blocks of lands, had still the same effect on the common folk--dispossession of what they considered to be the lands of their fathers. There is no record here of burnings and cruelty--only heartbreak and parting from the hills and glens which were dear to them and had been their homeland for centuries.

At the time of the 1829 emigration, the parish population is estimated as under 3000 souls, the far greater portion of them being located in the glens which debouch on Comrie, Glenartney with the Water of Ruchill, Glenlednock with the stream of the same name, and the valley of the Earn and Loch Earn itself. Most folk lived on farmtouns or crofts, and in the cots clustered around the farmsteads. It is only when we look at the scattered remains of settlements and examine the old Baptismal Registers, that we begin to realize how many folk were accommodated in those glens and on those hillsides.

By 1829, the village was beginning to grow and the small holdings in the glens were being given up, as the country turned over from mere subsistence farming to other ways of life. Many small crofts were vacated, the land enclosed, and larger farms created. It has been estimated that in the parish of Comrie, more than 5000 acres of Common land were enclosed. Sheep walks were opened up in the glens where the "wee, black cattle" of the Trysts of Crieff and Falkirk had pastured on the hills, great areas were given over to the creation of deer forests and game preserves. Of course, other influences were at work—pressure of population and basic hunger. With the defeat of Napoleon and the ending of the French Wars, came a tremendous slump in the demand for the products of the land. The vast armies and navies had been disbanded and the demand for the beef to feed them had disappeared.

Of course, as the small tenants and cottars moved out of the glens, they did not all take to emigration or to the large towns to the south. Many merely came down into the village where they continued with their cottage industries of weaving and dyeing. They created a very thriving community but time was not on their side, and with the rapid advance of the Factory System, they too, were overtaken by events, and during the 1840's this trade faded away. Again a large number took to the colonies, many now going to New Zealand and Australia. It can be said that the drain never ceased and goes on, even today, though numbers involved are few by comparison with the figures quoted for 1829. And who were these countrymen of ours who were taking this step into the unknown? We know who some of them were as their Petition to the Government of the day makes clear. It reads:

> To the Right Honourable Sir George Murray, Bart., Secretary to the Colonies the petition of the undersigned from the parish of Comrie and its vicinity:

Humbly Sheweth:

> That your petitioners are all mostly married men and possessed of families that in consequence of the pressure of the times they are inclined to emigrate to Upper Canada and they are all possessed of means sufficient to support themselves till such time as they can be supplied from the soil, and as a great part of them have been bred to the different branches of farming they are still inclined to follow the same profession. They therefore take the liberty of intruding on your Honour's more important duties as the only channel through which their wish can be obtained, and they humbly hope that your Honour will have the goodness to <u>furnish them with a letter to the Governor, or Deputy Governor of Upper Canada authorizing them to locate your petitioners on their arrival there with a grant of land.</u> Your petitioners having disposed of all their effects they are now ready for sailing sometime in the month of May.

Comrie 24th March 1829.

> May it therefore please your Honour to take the case of your petitioners into consideration & grant such relief as your Honour may deem most proper and your petitioners shall ever pray, &.

1. John McGregor wife & 5 children under 14 years of age.
2. Daniel Camron wife & 6 children under 14 years of age.

3. William McNiven wife and 6 children under 13 years of age.
4. Widow McGregor & family 6 children under 21 years of age.
5. Colin McNab Single.
6. John McEwen Single.
7. Duncan Drummond wife & 5 children under 14 years of age.
8. Alex Camron wife & 5 children under 21 years of age.
9. Duncan Comrie wife & 4 children under 17 years of age.
10. Daniel McEwen wife & 4 children under 12 years of age.
11. Robert Turner wife & 4 children under 11 years of age.
12. James McGregor Single.
13. Duncan Drummond Single.
14. Andrew Tainsh & wife.
15. James Nicolson & wife.
16. James Midlemas wife & 5 children under 12 years of age.
17. Duncan Camron Single.

Under the leadership of Duncan Comrie, the party of 78 souls boarded the brig at Greenock and, unlike most similar sailings which put into Quebec or Montreal, they landed at St. John, New Brunswick.

The party's onward journey was by coastal vessel into the mighty St. Lawrence to Montreal, where they rested a few days and were medically examined lest they might carry the deadly cholera which so often broke out in Britain in those days. Thence they travelled on foot to above Lachine where they again took boat or journeyed on foot by tracks cut through the dense forests to Lake Ontario. Onward again by boat to Coburg on the north shore of the lake and thence on foot to Rice Lake and the Otonabee River where they set to work on the lands allotted to them. The first need was for a cabin to provide shelter and then to clear an area of forest for the sowing of corn. It is hard to imagine the hardships and difficulties they endured in their first years. Only bit by bit could the dense forest be cleared. For long afterwards their only ploughland was encumbered by stumps of trees. Pasture for their few animals was limited to the lush grass which grew in the swamps. There was an abundance of wild life, wolves, bears and other denizens of the woods. Berries and fruits of all descriptions grew in profusion and the lakes and rivers teemed with fish. There never seems to have been any shortage of food, and timber for fuel was everywhere. Roads were non-existent and movement was by blazed trail through the trees or by canoe on the waters.

At all events, they eventually prospered in the next generations, as they never would have done in the old country. They had their own land and had no man to call "laird" or master. In time, small communities arose and served as centres for meeting their neighbours, for religious and educational purposes, for on these last two the Scots had set their hearts and minds as their fathers before them. Many of their descendants have risen to high positions in Church, State and in the Services.

The eldest child in the care of Duncan Comrie was Peter McIntyre, born in 1811 at Innergeldie, in Glenlednock. On the voyage over he often nursed on his knee, two year old Margaret Comrie, whom he eventually married in 1843. They had a large family of ten children whose descendants are scattered far and wide. In 1977 one of them, Melville McIntyre from Keene, Ontario, visited Comrie for a couple of days, when he was taken to view the scenes his ancestors had known, probably for centuries. His excitement was great when he saw for the first time the deserted croft of Tighnasithe, which he only knew from a letter written over a hundred years before. He carried home two roofing slates, or shingles as he called them. They now hang in a place of honour on the wall of his sitting-room. He has twice returned since that first visit.

It was a strange coincidence which, some years ago, brought my son in Montreal, a city of over two million people, into touch with a business client, who, on hearing his Scots accent, asked him where he came from in Scotland. Peter replied, "Oh! You'll never have heard of it. It's a wee place called Comrie, in Perthshire." His client answered, "Not only have I heard of it, but my folks left there, almost 150 years ago, in 1829." This was Malcolm McNevan, the name having undergone a "sea-change" in crossing the Atlantic. His emigrant ancestor was William McNiven whose name appears on the petition, along with his wife and six children under 13 years of age. William was not long to enjoy his new-granted acres in Upper Canada, for he died within six weeks of landing. His widow, with her strong pioneering spirit, had a long and hard struggle to bring up her brood in that forest wilderness, but she succeeded. Her sons, in their turn, took up farming and today descendants of the original settlers still farm the lands of their forebears.

The McNivens came from Glenartney and Blairnroar, from Achinner and Dalclathick. Indeed, one of the earliest recorded baptisms in the Parish of Muthill is that of Archibald, son of James McNiven and wife, Margret Ogilbie at Blairnroar on 12th November 1697. They were tenants on the Drummond estates of the Earl of Perth and in 1713, William McNiven in Dalclathick was ordered out by his Jacobite laird to carry arms for the Old Pretender.

The order, which leaves no doubt regarding the power of the Laird in those days, reads:-

"William McGruther, in Dalclaythick, you are hereby ordered to acquaint William McNiven, in the same town, and Alexander McGruther, in Dalchrown, to go along with you as officers to command the company of our men that is to come out of your glen, and all men are hereby ordered to obey your command on their highest peril, which you are to intimate to them, as you will be answerable to us, and this shall be your warrant.

"Given at Drummond Castle, the fifteenth day of August, one thousand seven hundred and thirteen years.

"See that none of the men of Auchinnear of whatever rank be absent, as they will be answerable, and all the men in good order.

"(Signed) DRUMMOND."

Many McNivens lie in the kirkyard of Tullichettle, a mile or so from Comrie, on the banks of the Ruchill.

A chance publication of an enquiry in an Ontario Genealogical Bulletin brought another enquiry from Jim McAndless of Toronto who wrote that he had long known that his ancestors came from Perthshire but from which part, he did not know. By a stroke of luck, when the farm of their original land grant was recently sold, the new purchaser, in putting insulation into the house attics, came on a bundle of old papers and letters, among which the following was one:

> "That the bearer John Carmichael with his wife Mary McLaren resided in this parish from their infancy behaving soberly, honestly and free of public scandal or ground of Church Censure, known here,
>
> That they are communicants and may be admitted into any Christian Society where providence shall order their lot–Is attested at Comrie this 10th. June 1818.
>
> > Patrick McIsaac. Minr.
> > John Drummond. Sess. Ck.
> > Alexr. McLaughlan. Elder
> > John Kennedy. Elder."

This simple "testificate", as it was often called, of Communicant membership of a Scots Presbyterian kirk, acted in much the same sort of way as a modern passport. It also let Jim McAndless know that his folk were from this parish of Comrie. John Carmichael was his great, great grandfather. A letter found at the same time was dated from Glentarken, a settlement now long deserted, high on the hills above the north shore of Loch Earn. Here, in the years 1755/56, according to the Reports of the Forfeited Estates Commissioners, for the Perth estates were again forfeit to the Crown after the '45, we find seven Carmichaels with their wives and families on their crofts. So, when Jim McAndless came here a few years ago, he found, not only his place of origin, but that he had distant cousins still resident in Comrie, and others whose names had been changed by marriage.

Again, a few years ago, I was visited by Mrs. Dorothy Dudley of West Hampton Beach, New York, who was well-briefed on her emigrant ancestors but wished to learn exactly whence they came. Though the locality has much changed since Peter Cram was miller at Milton, enough remains to show where he had his home and his mill. It was in 1820 that Peter Cram, his wife Janet Key and their seven children sailed on the Ben Lomond for Upper Canada, now Ontario, where they took over land in Beckwith Township, not far from the present town of Carleton Place (which incidentally, is named after Carlton Place on the south bank of the Clyde, in Glasgow), near the Rivers Ottawa and Rideau. The father and each of his four sons who were old enough, qualified for land locations of 100 acres each. Peter Cram of Milton and Janet Key of Monzievaird, both communicant members of the Secession Kirk of Comrie during the ministry of the Rev. Samuel Gilfillan, father of the church luminary of the day, George Gilfillan of Dundee, were the great, great grandparents of Dorothy Dudley. The extant Baptismal Records maintained by Mr. Gilfillan, show the baptisms of at least three of Peter Cram's children.

On 21st. July 1818, the brig "Curlew" put out from Greenock. On board she carried 205 persons, men, women and children from parishes neighbouring Comrie; from Comrie Parish she took away 95 persons. Among the passengers were Peter Cram's eldest son, John, taking with him his young bride Isabella Stalker of Tullibannocher. They settled in Beckwith Township and it was on their glowing reports that Peter and his family followed two years later. Incidentally, it was aboard the Curlew that Archibald Dewar, his wife and children sailed, leaving their croft in Glenartney, whither they had previously come from Killin, having in their possession the Quigrich, or Crozier of St. Fillan of Glendochart, of which his family had been the 'Dewars' or guardians for centuries. In 1876, Archibald's son, Alexander, with the consent of his son Archibald, transferred and surrendered the Quigrich to the Society of Antiquaries of Scotland "on trust to deposit the same in the National Museum of Antiquities at Edinburgh, there to remain in all time to come for the use, benefit, and enjoyment of the Scottish Nation."

By the strangest of circumstances the writer was asked three years ago by the present minister of Comrie Parish to answer, if possible, an enquiry from a Mrs. Isobel Squire Almassy, of San Jose, California. Her letter reads: "I have recently been given our Cram Family Bible and have copied the enclosed from the front of the Bible. I am wondering if your office might have records of Isabella Stalker that would pre-date 1800, the year I think she was born. I am particularly interested to know the place and date of her birth and that of her parents and grandparents if possible...I am the eldest grand-daughter of Isabella Cram, who is the grand-daughter of John Cram...and copied from the Family Bible:

John Cram's Family Register.

"Beckwith, the 6 of October 1825.

With a short but particular account of my Birth and Geneology, which may both be of satisfaction to myself and may be useful afterward to those who may yet spring from our loins when it is most likely they will become very ignorant both of land and the place of which Gave Their Predecessors Birth:– I was born in Milton in the Parish of Monivard on October 2, 1795 and was married on the 21 March 1818 to Isabella Stalker from Tolwannocker in the Parish of Comrie and in the year of our marriage was embarked from the land of our Nativity—and forever Bade Adieu to the Place which Gave us Birth. And became Settlers in the Forest of America where we are now. And Where God hath Graciously Pleased to Grant us the Following Children."

The questions asked were satisfactorily answered, not from any local Church Office Records for these are now in Register House, Edinburgh, but by two ancient gravestones in the Auld Kirkyard at Comrie.

So Dorothy Dudley of New York and Isobel Almassy on the opposite coast of America, in California, trace their roots back to Peter Cram and Janet Key of the joint parish of Monzievaird and Strowan which neighbours Comrie.

As I am deeply involved in this story of the Crams, I shall continue in more personal terms.

As I mentioned earlier, Dorothy Dudley was well-briefed on her emigrant ancestors and had in her possession a copy of her complete family tree. On my expressing admiration of this wonderful record, and some envy, she very kindly promised to send me a copy. This she did, making my knowledge of the Crams very considerable. I did not then think of the family tree as anything other than a souvenir of a pleasant meeting. How wrong I was!

About a year later, around eight in the evening, my phone rang and a voice said, "Are you David McNaughton? I understand you may be able to help me. My name is Harkness Cram from Connecticut, and I am seeking information on my ancestors." My reply was brief, "I do believe, Mr. Cram, that I know more about your ancestry than you do yourself." I could hear an audible intake of breath, and an urgent request. "When can we meet?"

Next day, the meeting took place, and it was exciting

Mel and Jean McIntyre of Keene, Ontario. Mel's ancestor, Peter McIntyre, was born at Invergeldie. He emigrated to Canada in 1829.

Harkness and Mary Lou Cram of Weston, Connecticut. Hark's ancestor, Peter Cram, being dispossessed from his mill at the Milton, emigrated to Canada in 1820.

for both parties. Harkness Cram was aware of his own descent from Peter Cram of the Milton, but he had no knowledge of any more distant relatives, equally descended. He had never heard of Dorothy Dudley, or of Isobel Almassy, and when he saw my copy of his family tree of all the descendants of Peter Cram, he was quite astounded. He returned to the States and immediately began correspondence with such members of his extended family as he was able to locate in the States and in Canada. The search has become an absorbing obsession for him. One of his first holidays was to the Carleton Place area of Ontario, where he found the Cram burial ground and the places where they had farmed; he also found a full cousin of whose existence he had previously been unaware. Finally, he planned a grand family reunion at his home in Weston, Connecticut. Since my wife and I were visiting our son in Quebec at that time, we were flown down to New York and entertained for a few days in Hark's lovely home in Weston. In his spacious gardens, in a temperature of 90 degrees the "Cram Clan Conclave" was celebrated by some thirty members of the family. Each one told of his descent from one son or another of old Peter Cram. My wife felicitously asked them to be mindful of those who had been their forebears and had fought the wilderness to make a livelihood. My part was easy, as I confined myself to a short explanation of the Clan system as it had been up to the '45, the reasons for the great emigrations to America, and the beauties and topography of Strathearn.

My wife and I were struck by two facts; that so many of these folk were still named Cram or had the name Cram as part of their baptismal names; that they were all still interested in their roots in Scotland.

But this is not the end of the story which is still unfolding. Only this summer a young woman called at my door and announced that she was Jennifer Cram from Newport News, Virginia. She, too, knew of her descent from Peter Cram but of other branches of

the family, she was unaware. And again this year
my son found in his phone book another Cram as professor in Montreal. But quite the most odd link of the
chain of this story was forged away in the forest lakeland
of Quebec, when, in an afternoon of driving rain and
wind, two persons knocked on the door of my son's
cottage by Lac de la Montagne Noire in the Laurentians.
It transpired that the lady was a Cram whose family
had left Carleton Place about 1890 and had lost all
trace of the other members of the family.

Somehow the tale of the Cram family and my relation-
ship with it tends to read like something of a story
book. Here we have a large family, scattered far
and wide over a continent, who trace their roots back
to the Parish of Comrie. How different would their
fate have been, had not Lord Balgray ordered the destruction of the mill at the Milton?

CHAPTER XVIII

KIRK SESSION RECORDS

There is much historical fact and interest hidden behind the lines of the old Kirk Session Minute Books. Not only were the Minister and Kirk Session responsible for the spiritual and pastoral oversight of the parish, they also acted as boards of managers in both local and National spheres. There being no Poor Law in Scotland, each parish was responsible for its own poor and on occasion, the poor of other parishes. All collections taken up on the Sabbath went into the Pocrs' box which was held in the hands of Boxmasters. The Box was also assisted by bequests, by fines imposed for moral lapses, and by the interest on loans to individuals made from the Box. In this work, as in much else, the heritors were conjoined with the Session. The Session was not averse from making raids on the Box, temporarily. For example, when there was need to build a loft to accommodate more folks, it was from the Box that the money came "to begin the work and quhatever money is disbursed be payd in again."

Action in smaller local matters was initiated by the Sessions themselves, based upon their experience and knowledge of the parish and its folks. In wider matters, intimations of countrywide, voluntary contributions would be passed down from the Privy Council itself, through the General Assembly of the Kirk, to Presbyteries and to Sessions. The Session undertook the uplifting of these voluntary collections at the kirk door and the forwarding of them to the Presbytery and onwards. It will be seen that this collecting of money for all sorts of purposes laid a heavy duty on ministers and Sessions to exhort kirk members to be regular in their attendance at diets of worship; otherwise the collections would suffer. There was a material as well as a spiritual purpose to be served in having the greatest possible turnout of the folks on the Sabbath.

Since there was no Poor Law, no Public Works Commissions, no Insurance Companies, great part of what is now the work of Government and other National bodies fell directly on the people themselves. Special voluntary collections were made for such purposes as building and repairing bridges and harbours, rebuilding of houses and even towns that had suffered from fire, the supply of goods and gear lost by fire or at sea. Money was needed, for example to relieve distress among seamen captured into slavery by the Turks or pirates of Algiers, for the support and maintenance of young men going through college to study for the ministry and for all sorts of purposes nowadays undertaken by Government or by the Red Cross and similar organisations.

In all of these, at one time or another, the parishioners of the Parish of Comrie were called upon to take their share and do their part. Much is made today regarding the apparent repressive nature of the actions of ministers and kirk sessions, but had they not been so eident about their duties, much general suffering would have been occasioned.

No modern passport had greater value and effect than the old system of testimonials or "lines" issued to parishioners in good standing. Not only did they allow, as now, admission to the Lord's Table, they were a certificate or in the old word "testificate" of a person's character and conduct. Without such a testimonial a man could not take up residence in a new parish, but needs must move on. At a later period in our Parish Kirk's history, the following was issued to intending emigrants from Comrie.

"That the bearer John Carmichael with his wife Mary M'Laren resided in this parish from their infancy behaving soberly, honestly and free of public scandal or ground of Church Censure, known here... That they are communicants and may be admitted into any Christian Society where providence shall order their lot -- Is attested at Comrie this 10th. June, 1818.

> Patrick M'Isaac, Minr.
> John Drummond. Sess. Ck.
> Alexr. M'Lauchlan. Elder.
> John Kennedy. Elder."

The Church of Scotland from the time of the Reformation directed strong efforts to producing a moral and orderly life among its folk. She was not merely concerned with teaching and preaching, she used stern measures of discipline, some of great severity, to achieve her aim.

When a name is first mentioned, the offender is accused of an offence or "delated". The following week, being summoned, he appears before the Session, and usually confesses and declares repentance. The matter may end up with a mere rebuke, but more often the sinner has to make repentance before the congregation. How often he has to do this depends on the gravity of his offence. For non-attendance at public worship or for Sabbath-breaking one such appearance may suffice, but for lapses of morality, three appearances are required. The guilty ones go to the "place of public repentance" or "the stool" or "the pillar", twice keeping silent and on the third appearance expressing repentance openly before being "absolved".

Those who were guilty of trilapse or quadrilapse or adultery or incest are severely dealt with. They appear in sackcloth before the Presbytery and express repentance. After appearing several times, similarly attired, before the congregation, they are referred back to the Presbytery. The General Assembly of

The one-time Parish Kirk of Comrie, built in 1805 — now the Youth and Community Centre.

1648 demanded 26 appearances for trilapse and for adultery, 39 for quadrilapse and relapse into adultery, and 52 for incest. The Session did not necessarily demand these appearances. Further to the "standing at the pillar" there was the rebuke from the pulpit.

Let us take a look at the Kirk Session Records of Comrie in the early years of the 18th. century. This will not be an exhaustive statement of all occurrences; rather it will be very selective and illustrative of the matters which concerned ministers and their folk in days gone by.

1700. 6 Sept. Mr. William Drummond late Schoolmaster of Culross presented the eldership a call to be schoolmaster, precentor and Session Clerk -- accepted.

1701. 18 May. Dft Disjunction presented to the Session showing that Achnashelloch, Culnacarrie, Finduglen, Carroglen, Lurg, Balmuick, Laggan, Milnmaik, Dunaverran, Drumachork, Coudouns, Meigers, and Trian are to be disjoined from Monzievaird and Strowan paroches to Comrie and all west of the Beach disjoined from Comrie and annexed to Balquidder.

16 Dec. "After prayers Sederunt Mr. John Campbell, moderator, James Campbell of Aberuchill, James Drummond of Comry, James Drummond of Drummondernoch, Alexr. Drummond of Balnacoul, heretors, the whole eldership & several parishioners".

1702. 5 Apr. "Sederunt Mr. John McCallum minr., William Comry, Jo: Drummond, Donald M'Intyre, John Stalker, John M'Claran, Duncan Morison, and Malcome Carmichell elders.
Drinking in taverns during divine service denounced.

1702. 20th Apr. Collected........................... 01-04-00.
given to Mary Philp, a poor woman........ 00-05-00.
given to Margt. Stalker, a poor woman....00-04-00.
given to M'Rorie's winding sheet............01-04-00.

1702. 28th Apr. Which day the minister, boxmasters and elders, by appoyntment of the session, having mett for sighting the box and noticeing severall things anent the church, they find in the box. 29-14-00.

whereof given to Pat. Comrie, Bedall, to compleat all house mealls resting to him preceding march last. 06-00-00.

given to the bursar.............................. 03-00-00. They agreed with Duncan Galoch to keep the roof of the kirk waterproof and to mend the bell house when it stands in need yearly for three pounds.

1702. 3rd May. Collected............................. 02-08-00.

1702. 4th May. maryed Patrick McNab with Anna McIlchonell; Duncan Stalker with Crystan Clark.

1702. 10th May. Collected.......................... 01-16-00. After prayers sederunt minr. and elders. Which day Duncan D. fornicator with Janet M., John C. fornicator with Kate G. and William M. fornicator with Kate M. being cited this day, called compeired and confest yr sin; exhorted each of them to serious repentance. The session appointed them to enter to the place of public repentance the nixt Lord's Day. Likewise John B. in Cultibragan, fornicator wt. Elizabeth G. being called compeired and confest guilt. The session ordained him to attend the session for that effect when cited yrto.

Given to John Mathie, a poor man......... 00-06-00.

1702. 17th May. Sermon at Dundurn and collected .... 00-16-00. which day Duncan D. appeared on the pillar 3to. (tertio) and payd fine for himself and party both being poor. 03-06-00.

Today John C. appeared on the pillar 2do. (secundo).

To judge from the considerable number of fines for irregular behaviour, the augmentation to the Poors' Box must have been great. How offenders came to the notice of Minister and Elders is not made clear, but doubtless more by information received and gossip than by witness evidence, except where the condition of the poor lass left no room for doubt.

1702. **14th June.** Collected........................ 01-02-00. The officer reported that he had summonded William M. and John B. to the place of public repentance according to appoyntment to this day, being cited, obeyed not. The session appoynted their officer to cite them to the pillar 2do. against this day 8 days.
given to Patrick Comrie, Bedall for shoos............
.... 00-16-00.
9th July. given to a blind stranger......... 00-02-00.
19th July. which day Katherine G. appeared on the pillar 3to. – absolved.
given to James Mathie, a poor man......... 00-12-00.
given to Wm. Symie recommended by the General Assembly................................ 00-18-00.

1702. **26th July.** The Session likewise appoynted Donald M. in Port, adulterer with Christian M. in Tullibannocher to be summoned to attend the Presbytery of Ochterardour the 28th July instant.
2nd Aug. Given for a sand glass to the kirk and carriage yrof................................ 00-12-00.

1702. Given for a session book.................. 01-16-00.

1702. **4th Oct.** Which day yr was intimation made of a collection for the relief of the town of Leith much whereof being burnt by an accident of pouder.
given to Kathie Bonnar as recommended by the Synod................................ 00-07-00.
An act of disjunction and amendation of paroches from the Commissioners for plantation of kirks...intimate from the pulpit.
....disjoin the lands of Achnashelloch, Culnagarrie and Findoglen in Glenartney from the united

paroches of Strowan and Monzievaird and annex to kirk and Parish of Comrie, and disjoin lands of Carroglen, Lurg, and Balmuick, Laggan, Miln of Maik, Dunabarran, Drumachork from Strowan and Monzievaird to Comrie and separate the whole land now within the Parish of Comrie lying bewest the Water of Beich on the north side of Locherne from the kirk and parish of Comry and annex same to the parish of Balquhidder and declare the foresaid annexations to be the only quoad sacra.

25th oct. given to the smith for a sneck to the kirk door and a lock to the latoran....01-00-00. given to Duncan Galoch for righting the pulpit and putting on the sneck with lead.......... illegible. *The Latoran was the lectern, the precentor's reading desk whence were read passages from the Bible before the entry of the minister to the pulpit. Perhaps the lock was for the pulpit bible which was often kept locked to the lectern.*

1702. **1st Nov.** given to Katherine Neish in Aberuchill
....

given to Patrick Carmichell, a cripple....
8th Nov. given to buy shoos for the poor of the parish.................................06-00-00.
15th Nov. given to John, a poor boy, to buy a book......................................
given to Patrick Comrie, Bedall for shoos
....

1703. **3rd Jan.** collected.........................02-00-00.
given to Elizabeth Drummond, a poor woman....
....
given for mending the kirk plate.............00-04-00.
10th Jan. given for the sark goon and makeing yrof...................................... 02-15-00.
given to M'inroy to buy shocs................. 00-12-00.
given to a poor scholar to buy a book......00-04-00.
given to Patrick Comrie, Bedall being long sick...00-06-00.

17th Jan. This dayes collection (01-04-00) given to Thomas Robertson in Glentarkin bedfast a long time.

given to Alexander M'Nab, boatman to buy four do alls to mend the boat.............. 02-00-00.

9th May. given to Duncan Drummond lying sick at the Carsehead being a parishioner...........

.... 01-00-00.

The Carsehead was along the S. Crieff Road, near the Lennoch.

given to a stranger....................... 00-01-00.

given to a blind stranger...................... 00-01-00.

8th Aug. The dayes collection (01-00-00) given to Duncan Galoch anent the mending of the roof of the kirk.

given for an hundred sclaits to the kirk

given for the horse bringing the sclaits

given for the two loads of lyme to the kirk

.... 02-00-00.

The session appoynted a meeting to be held amongst themselves to be at Comry the 4th. of November in order to the sighting of the box and taking an accompt of the condition of the poor.

1703. 4th Nov. Which day the Minr. elders and box-masters having taken an accompt of the money of the box they found therein.............. 56-00-00.

Out of which distribute to the poor to buy shoos..

.... 07-00-00.

given to pay the Bedall's house rent........ 02-00-00.

given to Robert Menzies recommended f rom Fortingall...................................... 00-06-00.

given to Margaret M'Gibbon, a poor woman........

.... 00-06-00.

given for the carriage of two letters to Edinburgh for the Irish Bibles........................ 00-03-00.

1704. 28th Jan. Which day...payed to the smith for the furniture of three big windows of the kirk....

.... 03-00-00.

given to the bursar...............................03-00-00.

30th Mar. Given to Mr. Grahame and his wife having suffered the loss of their goods coming from Ireland to Scotland by the French privateers as his testificate..............................02-18-00.

1704. 21st May. Marion M'C. appeared on the pillar pro secundo.

given to Janet M'C...a poor cripple.........00-09-00.
given to John Douglas once merchant in Dunblane having lost his goods by sea....................00-10-00.
given to John M'Come in Dunfermline having a palsie..00-03-00.
given a poor stranger with small children 00-02-00.

3rd June. which day Donald Cameron in Movie gave up his name in order to proclamation with Janet M'Claran in Ardveich both in this paroch.

4th June. Which day the session considering the necessitie of augmenting the numbers of the elders in the paroch did nominat a certain number of honest men of good report and for that end the minister was desired to commune with them upon that and report his diligence against the nixt Lord's Day.

Marion M'C. appeared on the pillar pro tertio and was absolved having formerly payed her fyne.

1704. 11th June. Which day the minister reported that he had comm23ned with the persons formerly nominat by the Kirk Session to be elders to wit Duncan Campbell in Milntoome, Duncan Drummond in Mewie, Alexr. fferguson in Port, Patrick M'Claran in Glentarkine Easter, John Carmichael in Glentarkine Wester, John M'Claran in ffinglen, John M'Coll in Ardvorlich, Duncan M'Ewan in Cussivaccan, John M'Mair in Meigor and Duncan Morison in Blairmore & finding them willing to accept that he desired them to attend the Session against this day, who compeiring before the Session were interrogat of their willingness to accept the office of eldership they unanimously consented. Whereupon the Session appoynted their edict to be served against this day eight dayes.

11th June. given for iron and for cutting William Comrie's seat to make way for upsetting the loft..00-06-06.

18th June. Edict of the elders served.

25th June. Edict of persons proposed for elders and there being no objections they were ordained.

6th Aug. Which day a strife being about a stool before Colin Campbell's seat for against the wester door belonging to Patrick M'Kissick in Meovie, Duncan M'Claren in Morell and Alexander M'Kinnis in Aberuquhill they condescended amongst themselves with the advyce of the minister and elders to prevent debate for the future that the said stool is to belong to the saids forenamed persones and yrs in all tyme coming each having a fourth part yrof.

Given to Janet Douglas a minister's relict having six children and her house having been burnt.......
.... 00-14-00.

20th Aug. Given to Duncan Galoch for two big windows and a little window, casements and brods yrto..05-00-00.

27th Aug. given to a poor boy named Lindsay......
.... 00-03-00.

given for iron and workmanship to make bands and snecks to the little window beneath the loft..00-14-06.

3rd Sept. given to Elizabeth Miller and her sister in Dalginross being both by an accident criples for the tyme........................... 00-19-00.

17th. Sept. given to John Gordon son to Alexander Gordon in Achnollis in the paroch of Glenmuick being cured of an extraordinarie disease. 00-06-00.

A voluntar contribution collected through the paroch to pay for cutting John S... a poor boy of the gravell and payed accordingly.......25-06-00.

1705. **18th Mar.** given to Duncan Graham recommended from Argyll.. 01-04-00.
given to Donald Mcillchrist in Ardownage having his son cut of the gravell...................... 00-12-00.
A collection intimate for repairing the Colledge of St. Andrews.

25th Mar. Which day the intimation of the ex-communication of James Anderson in the Paroch of Fossoway was read publicly conforme to the order of the presbyterie.

1705. **1st Apr.** Sr. James Campbell of Aberuchill was orderly proclaimed in order to marriage with Lady Jean Campbell daughter of the Earle of Loudoun.

2nd June Which day Malcolm McNeiving in Gualnacarrie in this paroch gave up his name in order to proclamation with Margaret McNeiving in Blairnroar in Muthill Paroch.

11th June Malcolm McNeiving having neither brought testificate for himself out of Dunblane paroch during his abode there nor his partie from Muthill paroch their proclamation thereupon delayed.

30th Sept. given to the bedall for shoes for gathering fog to the kirk......................00-16-00.

16th Dec. given to two broken merchants in Stirling...00-10-00.

1706. **12th Mar.** Donald Carmichael in Glentarkine & Elizabeth n'Cansh in Glaslarich gave up their names.

24th Mar. Donald Carmichael & Elizabeth n'Cansh yr. proclamation stopped by her parents.

7th April given to the bell tow.............. 00-08-00.
given to Christan Mcvorich a poor lass to buy a psalme book......................................00-09-00.

26th Apr. given to Mr. John A...for a student recommended from Aberdeen................00-03-00.

27th Apr. Duncan m'Ewan in Balmuick & Elizabeth n'Cansh in Glaslarich cried.

It is hoped that Elizabeth finally found the right man, agreeably to her parents. She does not appear to have wasted much time grieving over poor Donald.

1st Sept. collected for a bridge on Ruthven Water...01-04-00.

1st Dec. The session being informed that ther is one John Campbell a stranger come to Craggish having two wives appoynted their officer to cite him and William Morrison his land lord to session against the nixt Lord's Day.

The session considering that there were manie people in the paroch that want seats in the kirk, they judged it needful that a loft be built in the west end of ye kirk for their accomodation and that money be given out of the box to begin the work and quhatever moncy is disbursed be payed in again, when ye seats are sold to such parishioners as wants and accordinglie:-

Im primis given for jests to ye loft........ 10-13-04.
for bringing home these jests................. 00-16-00.
for cutting, squearing & setting up these jests in ye wall... 05-00-00.
for three pillars to support ye loft.......... 01-04-00.
for slocking ye earth to ye channell to these pillars.. 00-06-08.
for fourtie four deals to ye loft.............. 25-12-06.
for building ye loft................................ 12-00-00.
for seven pounds of iron........................ 00-15-08.
forrester fie for ye Timber of ye loft..... 00-04-08.
for nails to ye loft................................. 02-05-00.
for peats to dry ye deals........................ 00-08-00.

So that the whole money that was disbursed out of the Poors' Box amounts in qhole unto the sum of fiftie nine pounds, five shillings, ten pennies Scots money.   59-05-10.

Given to John Philp student at St. Andrews the half of the years bursary................. 01-10-00.

To meet at Comry on Monday nixt to agree with Duncan Galoch for putting up and building the Repentance stool.

1706. 8th Dec. "The session considering the necessitie of having a place for publick repentance and noe place being found soe proper as before the loft on the north side above Coline Campbell's desk. Therefore, seeing the samen will not prejudge the said desk nor any other, they appoynted Duncan Galoch wright in Comrie to put up the samen against the nixt Lord's Day".

1707. 25th Mar. Which day the minister and 4 of the elders having met and having taken of the Repentance Stool gave to Duncan Galoch, wright, for the samen.................................... 16-13-04.

signed W. McCallum Min.

W. Drummond Sess. Ck.

1707. 25th May "Which day the minister informed the Session that Alexander m'Gruther of Meigor desired an extract of his seat in the loft. Which desire the Session thought reasonable and therefore appoynted the clerk to give him an extract yrof with the first convenience in manner following. fforasmuch as the minister and elders having for the better accomodation of the paroch built a loft on the west side of the kirk of Comry, with the money of the Box of the paroch, which loft is sold and is to be sold to the parishioners who will buy the samen for themselves and theirs in tyme comeing. And accordingly Alexander M'Gruther of Meigor being an Heritor of the said paroch quoad sacra, be virtue of an act of the Lords for plantation of kirks of annexations and disjuctions of paroches bought the roume of the foreseat of the said loft on the south side which divides the foreseat in two equall parts the south part yrof belongeth to him, and payed therefore in to the box, fiftein pounds thirtein shilling four pennys scots and that beside payment to the wright for building the said seat Thairfore the Session hath Impoured and be thir .....impowers the said Alexander m'Gruther his wife, family or any in his name to enter to and possess the said seat, as it is limited, peaceably without any lett stop or impediment as yr. own propertie in all tyme comeing".

Given to Janet Miller a poor woman in Comry to buy butter for to make salve to herself...........
.... 00-06-08.

1707. **26th Oct.** "Mr. William Drummond Schoolmaster prescentor & Session Clerk considering yt. he should not have anie peaceable residence anie longer in the paroch by reason of ye out:ragious carriage of some of ye parishioners to him he Demitted his charge, which was accepted & he craving a Testificat of his own and his families good behaviour during yr. residence in the paroch to witt for seven years time preceeding Lambas last the same was granted whereupon considering ye necessitie of having one to succeed in ye said office they did appoint yt ye minr. advertise ye Heritors to meet att this place against Tuesday come a fourtnight both residing in ye paroch and non residing in order to nominate & Call one to be Schoolmaster".

1707. **11th Nov.** "Which day being appointed for Electing of a schoolmaster, precentor & Session Clerk compeired Alexander Drummond of Bailnacuill, James Campbell of Lawers, Robert Stewart of Ardvourlich, Sir James Campbell of Aberuchill, John Red of Cultebragan together wt. ye. Session who did nominate & Call Hugh Callum in Lennoch in ye. paroch of Strowan to be Schoolmaster prescentor & Session Clerk".

16th Nov. "Which day Hugh Callum being called to be Schoolmaster, prescentor & Session Clerk having given his oath de fideli was admitted to be prescentor, & Session Clerk whereupon ye. Minuts & Register of ye. Session were delivered to him".

1708. **14th Jan.** Giv'n to Janet Drummond a poor woman in the paroch............... 00-12-00.
Giv'n of charitie to one Margaret Drummond......
.... 00-06-00.
3rd. Oct. Given to Alexander Tossoch boatman in Comrie to repair ye. boat...............03-00-00.
22nd May "The said day An act of recommendatione of ye. General Assembly for a contribution in favour of Mr Alexander m'Cracken & the Presbyterian Inhabitants of Lisburn in Ireland their meeting house being burnt to ashes was read by ye. minister after Divine services & ye. peeple exhorted to extend again ye. next Lord's Day yr. charitie according to their severall abilities".

1709. **29th May** Coll: for Lisburn meeting house........
.... 02-01-00.
12th June Coll: for ye Protestant Germans (in London)........................... 02-08-00.
19th June Giv'n to Alexander Tossach Boatman in Comrie to help repair the boat. He being a poor man................................... 02-00-00.
3rd July Giv'n to John Drummond merchant in Comrie to change ye. Kirk Bason it being insufficient...........................01-04-00.
4th Sept. "Her Majesty's letters patent for a contribution in favours of these that suffered by fire in ye. head of ye. Canongate in Edinburgh
.... 02-11-00.
30th Oct. Giv'n to Patrick Drummond, Presbyterie bursar the halfe of ye. Bursarie............01-10-00.

1709. **24th Nov.** "The Session considering that the peeple concerned in the loft in the west end of ye. kirk are desirous that the menner of its division among them be registrate that all debates in after ages about it might be prevented,

The samine was agreed unto which is as follows.
The South Side of the Loft belongs unto the persons following. The first seat belongs unto Alexander m'Gruther of Miggor his airs & Assignays Having payed for building the samine as his proportione the sum of fifteen pounds thirteen shillings and four pennies scots money. 15-13-04.
The second Seat Belongs unto John Morison in Daiden, Duncan Morison in Blairmore, John Morison in Cuilt, Duncan Morison in Ross, Duncan Morison in Bailnadalloch, Donald Morison in Innergeldie Upper their airs & assignays. Having payed for building the same as their proportione the sum of Twelve pounds Thirteen shillings four pennies scots money. 12-13-04.
The Third Seat Belongs unto Hugh Cameron in Bridge-end of Easter Dundurn, Donald Cameron in Meuzie, John Cameron in Dundurn Wester their airs and assignays having etc. 10-13-04.
The ffourth Seat Belongs unto William Gewrner in Mellarmore, William Gewrner in Meuzie, Andrew Gewrner in Mellarmore their airs etc.
08-13-04.
The ffifth Seat belongs unto Patrick ffergusone in Nether Tullibanachar, Alexander fferguson in Portmore, Duncan fferguson in Dundurn Wester, John fferguson in Cultabragan, Patrick fferguson in Mellarmore, Donald fferguson in Comrie etc. 06-13-04.
The Sixth Seat Belongs unto John Drummond in Comrie, Duncan Galoch there, & Nill Drummond in Meuzie etc. 05-13-04.
The North Side of The Loft Belongs unto the persons following.
The First Seat Belongs unto John Drummond in Garrichrew etc. 15-13-04.
The Second Seat Belongs unto John m'Kuan in Glaslarich, Donald m'Kuan in Tienacroi, John m'Kuan younger in Glaslarich, Patrick m'Kuan

H

in Tienashiee etc. 12-13-04.
The Third Seat Belongs unto William Reddoch
in Laggan etc. 10-13-04.
The ffourth Seat Belongs unto John Drummond
in Meuzie, Patrick Drummond in Aberuchill
Wester etc. 08-13-04.
The ffifth Seat Belongs unto Donald M'Laran
in Mellarmore, Patrick M'Laren in Donira, and
Donald M'Laren in Innergeldie etc. 06-13-04.
The Sixth Seat Belongs unto James Bruce in
Aberuchill Easter etc. 05-13-04.
This is the price of the room of each seat in
the whole Loft distinct from the seats them-
selves".

In 1711, the Presbytery of Auchterarder paid a visit
and estimates were taken for the new manse required --
to be 46 feet in length over walls, 19 feet in breadth,
with offices, houses and yard-dykes thereunto belonging.
The tradesmen were John Ross who professed skill
in mason work and William Comrie in Wright work.
They were to be joined by two honest men viz. Duncan
Galloch and John Miller, indwellers in Comrie.

In the year 1712, the presbytery of Auchterarder
sat to consider the question of the apportionment
of sittings in the kirk of Comrie. That is the old kirk,
the one prior to the one of 1805, the White Church.
We find that sittings were allotted as follows.

Earl of Perth	34 feet
Aberuchill	17 feet
Duke of Atholl	12.4 feet
Lawers	11.11 feet
Comrie	11.5 feet
Strowan	8.3 feet
Monzie	5.11 feet
Cultibraggan	5.11 feet
Ardvoirlich	5.4 feet
Drummondernoch	1.3 feet
Balmacuin	0.10 feet

Amusingly, Dr. Wilson asks "how could each sit conveniently on "his own room", or how could the Laird of Balmacuin, family, etc., sit on ten inches?".

1712. April 1st. intimation was appointed to be made in all churches of the bounds for a voluntary collection for building the bridge of Comrie, the collection to be brought into the next meeting of the Presbytery. The bridge must have been built but a very poor job it must have been, as in 1728, the Rev. Andrew Muschett wrote to Col. Campbell of Aberuchill that "the bridge of Comrie being in such a tottering case that neither horse nor man have passage".

1747. "An Accott of the repairation of the Kirk Loft of Comrie & what money was laid out for the same.

Imprimis William M'Gruther of Meggar for repairing the flooring of the Loft and Loft Door paid five pounds seventeen shillings four pennies Scots money Agust or September Jaiviijc & fourty seven years. As his proportion for his seat in the Breast of the Loft South Side".

1747. April 5. Note in margin opposite this date "Which time Mr. Menzies was Sess: clerk Mr. Mallioch being deposed for sometime from that office".

1747. April 5. "Which time the Session being informed that Mr Matthew Mallioch Schoolmaster at Comrie was guilty of Severall Gross Immoralities, deposed the forsd. person and appointed John Sutherland, Charity Schoolmaster at Lochearn Eand to perform in his room during their pleasure." etc.

1772. 10th November.

Mr. Menzies, Min. of Comrie and Moderator of the Session represented that he had good grounds to believe that the school at Comrie would be vacant immediately by the resignation of Mr. McNab, late schoolmaster of the Parish, therefore as none of the heritors appeared in person or by proxy, Mr. Menzies, in concurrence with his Session, did and hereby do immediately elect Mr. Duncan Ferguson, Student of Philosophy in the University of St. Andrews as Schoolmaster, Precentor and Session Clerk.

signed. Robt. Menzies. Moderator.
Patrick McFarlane. Elder.
Donald McKuan. Elder.

Comrie, February 7th, 1792.

The school of Comrie, having become vacant by the resignation of Mr. Donald Ferguson, the late incumbent, the Heritors and Elders of the Parish of Comrie met this day to supply the vacancy, when they elected Donald McIntyre, Blairchory, President and William Brown, Clerk. Two candidates appeared and having been examined by Messrs. Scott and Baxter, Ministers, the meeting unanimously elected John Drummond present schoolmaster of Campsie to be Schoolmaster of the Parish of Comrie, and gave him the right to all the emoluments arising from that office.

signed. Donald McIntyre, President.
John Drysdale for Col. Robertson of Lawers.
James Glass for the Rt. Hon. Henry Dundas and for Colonel Campbell of Monzie.
William Brown for Strageath and Mr. Drummond of Comrie.
Donald McIntyre.
Donald Drummond of Balnadalloch.
Peter Drummond of Balnadalloch.

N.B. Mr. McDiarmid, Minister, being...owing to his bad state of health.

Comrie 8th Decr. 1787.

"The Session do hereby appoint that there be four shillings Sterl. paid hereafter for the coffins of such poor people, as may be supported from the poors funds."

Comrie 31st August 1788.

"The Session have unanimously resolved not to grant the use of the Mortcloth to any without paying the usual moiety of 2/6 Sterl. for each time into the poors funds."

Comrie 7th June 1789.

"The Session being met & constituted Isabell Drummond an unmarried woman in Comrie voluntarily compeard. & being interrogated if she had brought forth a child in uncleanness lately, acknowledged that she had, and being further interrogated who was the father of her child, declared that it was the Right Honble. Henry Dundas, Treasurer of the Navy. The Session closed with prayer."

Dundurn 14th June 1789.

"This day Isabel Drummond appeared before the congregation was sharply rebuked and ordered to continue her appearance."

Note. No steps appear to have been taken against Henry Dundas.

2nd Aug. 1789.

"As severals of the Elders had lately departed this life Edict for assumption of Alex. M'Innes in Findiglen, Duncan Carmichael in Upper Tillibanicher, James Gordon in Dalchonzie & Angus M'Diarmid in Ardstrostan, served."

Dundurn Dec. 13th 1789.

"James M'Nab in Ester Glentarken & James M'Annsh in Comrie to be made Elders and Edict served."

Comrie 5th August 1798.

Wm. Stewart Esq., of Ardvorlich, John Cowan of Ruchalside, Alexr. M'Lachlane at Malmuick, Duncan M'Naughton at Moril and Jas. Taylor & John Kennedy both in Comrie to be assumed Elders and Edict served."

Dundurn 3rd Nov. 1799.

Letters from Mr. Angus MacDiarmid Nephew of the Min. as to steps he had taken and Petition to J.P. (?) of Edinr. to relieve Comrie parish of founding laid down on the Bridge of Comrie in Summer 1798.

Comrie 26th Decr. 1805.

Announced by Minr. that Miss Margaret M'Gruther daughter of Dr. Duncan M'Gruther late of Miggor &

Drummond Earnoch who was interred in the family burying place within the Churchyard of Tullichettle on Decr. 22nd. 1801 had bequeathed to the poor of the parish of Tullichettle £10 Stg. which sum, agreeably to her will, had been transmitted to the Minr. upon her mother's death.

Note: In 1829 a census was made by Elders which showed population of the Parish to be 2707.

CHAPTER XIX

PLACE-NAMES IN UPPER STRATHEARN

The great majority of names of places, rivers and hills in the district are of Gaelic origin. Their interpretation is no easy or even, perhaps, a wise venture, as often scholars are at odds as to their precise root and meaning. However, as it is felt that these names are of some interest to many people, some attempt should be made at their interpretation as, being largely topographical, they serve to show what features of the countryside attracted the attention of our forebears.

The names are taken from the Ordnance Survey maps and as these were compiled by surveyors, often English, with little or no knowledge of the Gaelic language, many inaccuracies of spelling have crept in. When the maps were first compiled in the mid 19th century, Gaelic, as a spoken language here had largely died out. Furthermore, Perthshire Gaelic was not of the high order of the tongue of the west and the Isles. Recourse has been had to early maps, particularly that of James Stobie of 1783, but the place-names here are mainly of farmtouns and crofts.

No claim is made that these interpretations are final and definitive. They will be subject to challenge by experts. They are recorded here because of their interest to admirers of this beautiful country and because they explain by their nature so many of its features, and its history.

Place-Names...

ABERUCHILL — Obair-Ruchail; confluence of the Ruchill with the Earn. The site of the castle is irrelevant; the estate ground comes to the confluence.

ACHADH — field, plain, meadow.

ACHADH RAINICH — field of fern or bracken; from Raineach, fern; genetive rainich.

ACHINNER — field at the junction of two rivers or streams; achadh, field, and inbhear; inver, confluence.

ACHRAW — achadh, field; raw, perhaps from ramh (pronounced rah) Gaelic for oar, but in Perthshire Gaelic used often for branch, tree, wood. East from Achraw along north Lochearn are place-names signifying birch and oak woods.

AIRIDH A'CHREAGAIN — shieling of the rocky place; airidh, summer pasture or shieling; creagan, little rock, rocky place.

ALLT NA-H-ATHA — burn of the kiln; al, allt, ault, burn or stream; ath, atha kiln.

ALLT na BEALACH CAR — stream of the winding pass; bealach, pass, glen, gorge.

ALLT A' BEALACH BHA AIRIDH — stream of the Pass of the Cows' summer pasture.

ALLT BHACAIDH — obstructing burn.

ALLT A' BHRAONAICH — stream of the drizzling rain.

ALLT NA CAILLICH — burn of the old wife, carline.

ALLT CEANN DROMA — stream of the head of the ridge.

ALLT NA CEARDAICH — burn of the smithy.

ALLT CEILIDH — burn of the visiting or pilgrimage.

ALLT A' CHALTUINN — burn of the hazels.

ALLT CHEAPAIDH — burn of the intercepting.

ALLT A' CHOIRE BHUIDHE — burn of the yellow corrie.

ALLT COIRE A' CHOIRE — burn with a corrie or whirlpool within a corrie.

ALLT CREAG NAN EUN — burn of the crag of the birds.

ALLT NA CREIGE DUIBHE — burn of the black crag.

ALLT AN CRICHE — stream of the boundary or march.

ALLT DHEACAIR ATH — perhaps should have read - allt an ath dheacair, burn of the terrible ford.

ALLT NA DROCHAIDE — burn of the bridge.

ALLT DHUNAIN — burn of the little fort or mound.

ALLT EAS AN AOIN — perhaps should read - eas nan eun, burn of the waterfall of the birds.

ALLT NA FEAGAN — burn of the notches, or offences.

ALLT NA FEARNA — burn of the alders.

ALLT NA FAING — burn of the sheep fank.

ALLT FHIANTAGAN — burn of the black heathberry.

ALLT FHUARCHOIS — burn of the cold hollow.

ALLT AN FHIONN — (pronounced un yowan), burn of the chief.

ALLT NAN GABHAR — burn of the goats.

ALLT NA GAISGE — burn of valour, or burn of the slope.

ALLT NA GALLANAICH — probably allt gallanach, burn full of branches.

ALLT IARUINN — burn of iron.

ALLT AN INNEIN — burn of the anvil.

ALLT AN IOGAIN — burn of the bird's claw.

ALLT A' MHIADAIR — burn of the meadow of grassy plain.

ALLT MOR NAN SPEIR — big burn of the sparrowhawk.

ALLT A' PHRIS GHAIRBH — burn of the rough thicket.

ALLT A' PHUIRT BHEG — Littleport Burn.

ALLT AN t-SEILICH — burn of the willows.

ALLT SGAIRNICH MHOIR — burn of the great scree.

ALLT SHIOS — Easter Burn.

ALLT SHUAS — Wester Burn.

ALLT STOB MILL — burn of the stump (stob) of shapeless hill (meall).

ALLT SHRATH A' GHLINNE — burn of the strath of the glen.

ALLT TAMHAISG — (now pronounced Altanish), burn of the spectre; should have read Tannaisg.

ALLT TOBAR SNEACHDA — burn of the snow well.

ANABA — ath na ba, ford of the cow. (Ford of the cows would be ath nam bo. Perhaps an example of corruption creeping in).

AODANN MHOR — great brow of the hill.

AONACH GAINEAMHACH — sandy hill.

ARDTROSTAN — height of Drostan. Drostain was one of the Celtic saints.

ARDVORLICH — ard-mhurlaig, promontory of the sea-bag. i.e. little bay in the loch.

ARREVORE — airidh mhor, big shieling or summer pasture.

ATH NA MEINE — kiln of the ore or metal.

ATH NAN SOP — ford of the wisps of hay.

AUCHINGARRICH — place of roughness. Many Gaelic words begin with gar or gair indicating roughness of some sort. Gairbheal means quarry, or in Perthshire, freestone. The reference may be to the stone quarry here, from which many Comrie buildings have been constructed.

AUCHNASHELLOCH — achadh an-t-seilich (pronounced achantyeelich), field of the willow copse.

BAD NA BEITHE — birch copse.

BAILE A' CHNOIC — farm of the hillock.

BALIMEANACH — Balmenoch, baile, farm, meadhonach, middle, middle farm.

BALLIG — lig may be from leac, meaning slab-stone and have reference to the stones of nearby Clathick. Or, the place on the declivity.

BALLINDALLOCH — farm in the meadow or riverside haugh.

BALMUICK — farm of the swine, muc, a pig or sow, muick, of pigs.

BALNACOUL — the site in the corner, or back-lying.

BALNAILT — the site, farm on the stream.

BEALACH BAILE NA CUILE — pass to Balnacoul.

BEALACH BEAGLARAICH — pass of the little ruin.

BEALACH BHA AIRIDH — pass of the cows' summer pasture.

BEALACH A' CHLAIS EALLAICHEAN — pass of the cattle track.

BEALACH A' CHOIRE RIABHAICH — pass of the drab corrie.

BEALACH A' CHOIRE RUCHAIN — pass of the wind-gap corrie.

BEALACH AN DUBH CHOIREIN — pass of the little dark mountain hollow.

BEALACH GHLIOGARSNAICH — pass of the tinkling noise.

BEALACH RUADH — red pass.

BEALACH AN t-SAGAIRT — pass of the priest.

MOR BHEIN — great mountain. (False Gaelic for Beinn Mhor).

BEINN BHAN — White hill.

BEINN BHEARNACH — mountain abounding in clefts.

BEN CLACH — Stoney mountain.

BEINN DEARG — Red mountain.

BEINN DOMHNUILL — Ben Donald.

BEINN FUATH — mountain of the spectre.

BEN HALTON — Beinn challtuin, hazel ben.

BEINN LIATH — grey mountain.

BEINN ODHAR — dun mountain.

AM BINNEIN — pinnacle, high conical hill.

AM BIORAN — the pointed or sharp one.

BIORAN BEAG — the little sharp one.

BLAIRHOORIE — Juniper field; perhaps from iubhar, juniper which grows extensively in Glenartney, so much that the description "Juniper Forest" has been applied.

BLAIRMORE — big field.

BLAIRNROAR — place of violent attack, incursion; Gaelic, Blar an ruathair. Perhaps an echo of the tradition of a fierce attack by the Caledonians on the Roman camp of Dalginross, or Blar-an-raoir, ground of the out-field.

BLAR DEARG — red field, field of blood. (May have reference to the attack mentioned above) or, possibly, the soil appeared reddish when name given.

BOLTACHAN — might be from botachan, mounds, or from bothach, a Perthshire word meaning marsh. (Lord Cockburn, on a visit to Lord Melville at Dunira speaks of taking a walk 'up the Badachan'.).

BONAWE (BRAE) — foot of the ford. The place is where a ford crossed the Earn, now bridged, at Dalchonzie.

BOVAIN — both meadhoin, middle stead.

BOWALKER — upper bothy, Gaelic bot uachdar, pronounced bawoochker.

BRAINCROFT — perhaps braigh na croite, upper part of the croft.

CARN CACHAILEITH LIATH — grey cairn by the break in the wall.

CARN CHOIS — cairn of the cavern, or crevice.

CARN NAN CLAISEAN GUAIL — cairn of the little coal-pits.

CARN LABHRUINN — Laurin's Cairn.

CARN LIATH — grey cairn.

CARN LUIG BAINNEACH — cairn of the milk-producing hollows.

Place-Names...

CARROGLEN — glen of the sheep, caora.
CAS DUBH — black foot, shaft of dark ground.
CLATHICK — place of the stones, clachaig.
CLUAIN — meadow.
CNOC BRANNAN — St Brenaind's knoll.
CNOC A' CHROCHADAIR — hangman's hillock.
CNOC A' MHADAIDH — hillock of the wild dog.
CNOC RIABHACH — brown, drab hillock.
CNOC NA SITHE — knoll of the conical hill.
CNOCAN DUBHA — little dark hillock.
COCHLADOW — perhaps from cachlaidh, a form of cachaileith, Perthshire Gaelic for break in the wall for cattle + dubh, black.
COILCAMBUS — wood at the bend or turn.
COILLE BAILE A' MHAOIR — wood of the farm of the maor (officer of justice).
COILE CRICHE — wood of the march.
COILEMORE — big wood.
COIRE BUIDHE — yellow corrie.
COIRE NA CLOICHE — corrie of the stone.
COIRE NA COMHAIRIDH — corrie of the shieling held in common.
COIRE DUBHGHLAS — dark grey corrie.
CORRIE AN EICH — corrie of the horse.
COIRE AN FHAIDHE — corrie of the seer, soothsayer.
COIRE NA FIONNARACHD — corrie of the cool breeze.
COIRE A' GOINEAN — corrie of the withered grass.
CORRIE GORM — green corrie.
COIRE AN LOCHAIN — corrie of the little loch.
COIRE NA MOINE — corrie of the moss.
COIRE NOCHD MOR — bare and high corrie.
COIRE NA RAINICH — corrie of the bracken.
COIRE RIABHACH — brindled corrie.
COIRE AN t-SLUGAIN — coire of the gorge.
COMRIE — cuimrigh. Comar meeting of the waters, a ruith, flowing.
CORNOCH — curled like a horn.
COWDEN — hazel.
CRAGGAN — rocky place.
CRAGGISH — creag, crag-innis, haugh land. (Relates to old Craggish. Present Craggish was once Ross Farm).
CREAGAN SOILLEIR — shining rocky place.
CRAIGNEICH — craig of the horse.
CRAPPICH — perhaps wooded from craobhach.
CREAG AN AONAICH — craig of the heath, moor, desert place, fir (Perthshire) according to site.
CREAG NA H-AIRIDHE — craig of the sheiling.
CREAG BEINN NAN EUN — craig of the hill of the birds.
CREAG BHALG — creag a'bhuilg, craig of the bag, or belly shape.
CREAG NA BEITHE — craig of the birch
CREAG A' BHUIC — craig of the buck.
CREAG BHUIDHE — yellow craig.
CREAG A' CHARUINN — craig of the rowan tree.
CREAG A' CHASAIN — craig of the path or road.
CREAG CHORRACH — steep crag.
CAM CREAG — creag cham, crooked crag.
CREAG A' CHRUIDH — crag of the cattle.
CREAG DHUBH — black crag.
CREAG NA DRONNAIGE — crag of the ridge summit.
CREAG DHUBH NAN EARB — dark crag of the roes.
CREAG EACH — crag of the horse.
CREAG AN EARARAIDH — crag of the searching.
CREAG NAN EUN — crag of the birds.
CRAG AN FHITHICK — Raven's crag.
CREAG NA GAOITHE — crag of the wind.
CREAG GHARBH — rugged or rough crag.

194

CREAG GHORM — blue crag.
CREAG IOCHDAIR — lower crag.
CREAG IOLAIR — eagle crag.
CREAG NA H-IOLAIRE — eagle's crag.
CREAG LIATH — grey crag.
CREAG AN LOCHAIN — crag of the little loch.
CREAG LOISGTE — parched crag.
CREAG MACRANAICH — perhaps, clear rock of the echoing cavern?
CREAG-MEACAN — rooty crag?
CREAG MHOR — big crag.
CREAG MHULLAICH — rock of the top, summit.
CREAG NA MOINTEICH — crag of the peat moss.
CREAG ODHAR — dun crag.
CREAG NA H-OISINN — crag of the corner, nook.
CREAG AN T-SEILISDEIR — crag of the sedge.
CREAG NAN SIONNACH — crag of the foxes.
CREAG AN T-SITHEAN — crag of the fairy hill.
CREAG THARSUINN — the cross, or oblique craig.
CREAGAN BAD AN FHITHICH — little crag of the copse of the raven.
CREAGAN A' PHULEIR — pillar crag.
A' CHREAGAN CEANNAN — little bald crag.
CUILT — nook, secluded place.
CULLOCH — nook; cuileach, angular (Perthshire Gaelic).
COISHAVACHAN — Gaelic cois has some connection with cas, foot. Probably the complete name here was an cois a'bhacain. at the foot or near the steepness of the ground.
CURROCHS — a marshy place.
DALCLATHICK — dal, meadow and clachach, stony.
DALRANNOCH — dal, meadow and raineach, fern or bracken.
DALVEICH — birch meadow, dale or field; bheithe, birch.
DERRY — grove or thicket, from doire, oak-copse.
DOIRE A' CHINN — from an doire a' chinn, grove of the head or of the chief.
DROCHAID CEANN DROMA — bridge of the end of the ridge.
DRUIM CHONNAIDH — firewood ridge.
DRUMLOCHLAN — from the site, 'lochlan' might come from lochbhlein (bh silent), meaning the flank of an animal or side of anything.
DRUMCHORK — oat ridge.
DRUMMONDERNOCH — ridge of the Earn which flows parallel, and ach, place-name suffix.
DRUMNACHORAN — ridge of the rowans; caorunn, rowan tree.
DRUM N' TOKEL — pronounced here as Drumshochle, probably Druim siogail - rye ridge.
DUBH-CHOIREIN — little dark hollow.
AN DUNAN — the little fort.
DUN AN AON DUINE — the fort of one individual.
DUN CAOCH — empty, blind, fort.
DUNDURN — fort of the fist (duirn).
DUNIRA — fort of the west ford.
DUN SLEISH — fort of a thigh-shape. (Slias, pronounced slaysh, thigh).
DUNTARVIE — for dun-tarbhaidh, from tarbh, a bull.
EAS AN AOIN — waterfall of the country.
EAS A' BHALTAIR — Walter's waterfall.
EAS AN LUB (luib) — waterfall of the marsh.
EDINAMPLE — oadann ambuill, face of the vat. Reference probably to the falls of Edinample.
EDINCHIP — hill-face of the block (plateau-like lump of hill, as here).
AN T' EILEAN — the island.
EILDREACH — probably should be eilidach or eildach - abounding in hinds.
ESCULLEN — waterfall of the holly. (eas and cuilionn, holly).
FEADAN DUBH — black wind-pipe or gap.
FINDUGLEN — findoglen, probably connected with fionn, a degree of coldness.
FINTULLICH — fionn-tulach, as above with tulach, tulaich, a knoll, little green eminence.
FUAR CHOS — cold hollow.
GARADH CRUAIDH — garadh, cave and cruaidh, hard. Perhaps should read garradh cruaidh, unproductive garden.
GARRICHREW — or gerrichrew; garbh, rough, uneven, broad, and ceathramh, a fourth (land

measure).
GLASCORRY — glas-choire, grey or green corrie.
GLASDALE — glas-dail, grey or green dale, meadow.
GLENARTNEY — very uncertain; perhaps gleann artain, glen of little houses, a clachan. Locally called Glenairten.
GLENBEICH — birch glen.
GLEN A' CHROIN — perhaps from crann (gen. croinn) meaning plough or tree.
GLEN FHUAR-CHOIS — phuar-chois, glen of the cold hollow.
GLEN GOINEAN — goinean in Perthshire, couch-grass or withered grass.
GLENTARF — tairbh, of a bull.
GLENTARKEN — pronounced locally as glentyarken. Hence probably from tearc, cow in Perthshire.
GUALANN LAOIGH — calves' shoulder (of land). Most crofts had a "calfies' park".
INVERGELDIE — at the mouth of the Geldie burn, from geal, bright, shining.
KEPLANDIE — Head of a marsh.
KINDROCHET — Bridgend; ceann drochaid.
KINGARTH — earlier pronounced Kingairt. Head of the cornfield.
LAGGAN — little hollow.
LAGAN RHUIDLEACH — winding hollow.
LAWERS — labhar, Lawers, is the name first of a stream, then of a district. The plural arises as there were three Lawers, L. Shios, L. Shuas and L. na craoibhe, Lawers of the tree. Labhar is from labaros, loud.
LEACANN NAM BAD DEARG — slope of the red thicket.
LEACANN BHUIDHE — yellow slope.
LEACAN DUBHA — dark slopes.
LEATHAD NA SGEITH — brae of the dirty effluents.
LECHKIN — from leacann, pronounced lyechg-unn, a sloping side of a hill.
LENNOCH — leana, meadow, swampy plain: in Perthshire, field of luxuriant grass.
LINN HULLOCH — linne, pool below a waterfall and a'chullaich, of the boar.
LOCHAN NA MNA — little loch of the woman.
LOCHERLOUR — luachair, rushes, and lour from lar, lair, of low ground.
LURG — ridge of a hill gradually declining into a plain, shank.
MAAM — slow rising hill, a hill pass.
MAILER BEAG — mailer, rent-paying farmer, hence the farm, and beag, little.
MAILER FUAR — as above and fuar, cold.
MAILERMORE — as above and mor, big.
MEALL A' CHOIRE RIABAICH?? — hill of the drab corrie.
MEALL CLACHACH — the rocky hill.
MEALL NA FEARNA — hill of the alders.
MEALL NAM FIADH — hill of the deer.
MEALL FIODHAIN — possibly "wooded hill".
MEALL NA H-INNEIN — hill of the anvil.
MEALL NA H-IOLAIRE — hill of the eagle.
MEALL A' MHADAIDH — hill of the dog, or wolf.
MEALL NA MOINE — hill of the bog or morass.
MEALL REAMHAR — round lump of a hill.
MEALL NAN SAIGHDEARAN — hill of the soldier.
MEALL AN T-SEALLAIDH — hill from which the view is obtained.
MEALL SGLIATA — Slate hill.
MEALL TAIRBH — bull's hill.
MEALL NAN UAMH — hill of the caves.
MEIGGAR — from migear, a boggy, marshy place: mig, a bog.
MILNTUIM — mill on the hillock.
MONADH MOR CHILLE — big moor of ruddle (red ochre).
MONADH ODHAR — dun-coloured moor.
MONADH A' PHUIRT MHOIR — Portmore moorland.
MONADH AN t-SRUITH BHAIN — moor of the white stream.
MONTELLIE — Mon (ADH, silent), tilly (tulach), upland with a knoll.
NEAD AN FHITHICH — raven's nest.
OCHTERTYRE — uachdair thir, upper part of the land.
PAIRC MHOR — the big park.
QUOIG — fifth part.

Melville Square, Comrie, from approach to Dalginross Bridge. Toll road system in operation then. Note the toll gates, R. and L. of roadway. Note, too, the observatory on roof of Brough's shop.

The village of St. Fillans, midway through the 19th century.

Place-Names...

RIONNAG — star.
SGAIRNEACH MOR — a big scree.
SGIATH AN ATH — Sgiath, wing or shield + ford.
SGIATH GORM — Sgiath, wing or shield + blue.
SGIATH A' PHIOBAIRE — Sgiath, wing or shield + piper.
SGOR RACINEACH — rounded hill with furrowed surface.
AN SITHEAN — the fairy hill.
SLIABH NA MEINNE — hill of the mine, or vein of metal.
SLOC CARG — terrible hole or den.
SPUT A' CHLEIBH — water fall of the creel. (A superb salmon leap of the Ruchill. Locally known as Dalness Spout.)
SPUT DUBH — black spout.
SPUT ROLLA — probably Rolla is a personal name.
AN T-SREANG — the line, or the ridge.
SREANG NAM BEITHE — the string of the birches.
SRON — nose, headland running from a mountain to a strath.
SRON AILEACH — airy.
    BAD AN FHEIDH — copse of the deer.
    BHUIDHE — yellow.
    NAM BROIGHLEAG — of the whortleberry.
    NA CABAR — of the caber or rafter.
    GHARBH — rough.
    NA LEACAINN — of the mountain-side.
    MHOR MHIC LAURAINN — great slope of McLaren.
    NAN SEARRACH — of the foals or colts.
STIOL NAN TARBH — the bulls' ropes, chains.
STRAID — a street, or row.
STROWAN — struie, a current or stream, srutnan, a streamlet.
STRUIE — from struthach, current place, struthaigh, whence Strowie, now Struie.
STUC NA CABAIG — pinnacle of the pillory.
STUIC A CHROIN — pinnacle of the poughshare.
STUC AN FHORSAIR — pinnacle of the (deer) forester.
TEYNRIACH — tigh + an + fhraoch, house of the heather.
TIGHNABLAIR — house in the field (blar).
TOM A' CHAISTEIL — castle-hill or mound.
TOM A' CHESSAIG — St Kessog's Knowe or Knoll.
TOM A' CHOIN — hillock of the dog.
TOM NA DAOICHE — hillock of the periwinkle.
TOM NA H-EISE — hindersome hillock. Or perhaps a mis-spelling of na h-easa, hillock of the waterfall.
TOM NAN IOLAIR — knoll of the eagles.
TOM A' MHINN — knoll of the kid.
TOMANOR — old map shows Toum e Noir, hillock of gold.
TOMRANNICH — ferny hillock.
TORLUM — bare hill.
TRIAN — third part.
TROWAN — an t-sruthain, streamlet.
TULLICHETTLE — tulach, mound and eadal, spoil or advantage. Mound of (some kind of) advantage.
TULLIBANNOCHER — tulach, hillock and beanchor, great horned bend. Hence, the hillock on the great horned bend "of the river".
TYNACROY — tigh na craoibhe, house of the tree.

CHAPTER XX

THE CHANGING SCENE - A PERSONAL VIEW

At the beginning of this century, the Parish and Village of Comrie presented a very different face from what they wear today, both in respect of the environment and the folk who have their homes here. A very high proportion of the inhabitants, other than the farm-workers who were forever on the move in search of better "fees", was descended from the original stock, and apart from the gentry, showed little difference from their forebears of even two centuries before. Which is not to say that they were uncouth or uneducated - far from it. Sadly, the Perthshire Gaelic of two centuries before had died out, though it was still spoken by some. My Grannie who was born in Glenlednock in 1833 had the Gaelic and even at the end of the 19th. century, Communion in Gaelic was still held here. The Kirk and the school had brought the folk forward, · while their innate intelligence allowed them to stand on their own feet in any sphere. Education stood in high regard and disputation in matters religious or political was eagerly indulged in. Many were weavers and every weaver's shop was a little parliament. In the main, one would say that they were good folk with little or no bent towards crime, save perhaps, to poach the odd salmon or rabbit. These were only crimes in the eyes of the lairds and the Law. The people were much given to self-help, while holding out a charitable hand towards any in need. There was no call then to bar and bolt doors, and one could walk safely without fear of molestation, both by day and by night.

Our three streams, Earn, Ruchill and Lednock, coming together at a nodal point, have not only given the place its descriptive name, but have settled the position of the village and imposed upon it its shape. We have the three entities, indeed not so long ago treated as three villages with separate population statistics, Comrie, Dalginross and The Ross. They are very separate and distinct. But how separate they must have been a mere two hundred years ago, when there were no bridges crossing the waters, and recourse had to be made to fords, often rendered treacherous in times of spate.

In my time, the folk in The Ross always spoke of "gaun ower tae Dalginross," and I know some Dalginross folk today who speak of "gaun doon tae Comrie", or "doon tae the Toll". Comrie folk seem very conscious of place and direction and frequent use is made of points of the compass - aist and wast, north and sooth. This makes it rather difficult for strangers who have not yet located themselves in relation to the sun. Now this peculiarity of ours is nothing new - it has been so for a very long time. A hundred years ago in 1881, McAra records that the denizens of Comrie had a curious, uncouth drawl and mode of expressing themselves, such as, "Are ye gaun tae Dalginross ower?" or "East at Lawers there wast". In 1834 John McLaren, the public crier of Comrie delivered himself of the following proclamation, "A tear o' shearers wanted; neither at Auchinshelloch up, nor Mailermore wast; Sandy Morrison's auld, rashy parks; fine rank corn, thruppence the thrave; three fill-fous o' the parritch and the braxy, and a' the rest o' yer meat."

In the early years of this century, this was a very isolated place. The railway had not long been extended from Crieff, being opened to traffic in 1893, and the line to St Fillans was quite newly built. The coming of the trains spelt the demise of the Crieff to Comrie coach - the Comrie Dasher. The station as I remember it, seemed a very hive of activity. Goods and passenger trains arrived and departed regularly. Nearly all goods traffic, the mails and coal came here. There were fewer trains so bonnie as those of the old Caledonian Railway - engines in Royal Blue livery and the coaches in cream. Even the staff were memorable figures - do you mind of John Bull, the stationmaster, otherwise Mr Taylor, a kenspeckle figure and a man of standing; Jock McGregor the goods porter and Tam Macpherson, the passenger porter with his helpful, unfailing advice of "Change at Crieff Junction for Edinburgh." Crieff Junction had not then blossomed into the once magnificent Gleneagles Station. D'ye mind of Jock Gow, the lorryman, who, poor fellow, used to ease his bunions by cutting great holes in his boots? Then, too, there was Mr Duncan Comrie and his lumbering station bus, on whose back step, out of sight of the driver on the dickie, we would hitch a ride, till some bystander would cry out, "Wheep ahint, the cuddie's blind", when the tip of the whip would curl over the roof and lead us to a hurried departure. A journey then, to Glasgow or Edinburgh, was to a far-off place, not to be undertaken lightly, and almost a reason for putting one's affairs in order before departure.

Our pleasures may have been few, but such as they were they were eagerly expected and cherished when they came. The annual Sunday School picnic to St Fillans to Murdo Nicholson's field at Ardtrostan, all of five miles away, seemed the greatest treat in the world. Even today, when I see "The Crocodile" I can be back in those happy days. We U.P. Kirkers always travelled by train, even on occasion as far as Lochearnhead to Glen Ogle. How I envied the Free Kirkers and the Auld Kirkers who often went by farm cart! That would have been bliss! We are never satisfied.

Someone, long ago, I have forgotten who, wrote, "O! to be a boy again, to climb trees and throw stones in the water." Comrie was an enchanted place to grow up in, and for all I know, still is.

Another great event was the School Christmas Tree which was set up in the Qualifying room. This was in days before Comrie had electric power and the great tree was festooned with live candles which gave off not only a glorious light but also great heat. Safety was in the capable hands of Mr John Gilbert who moved around the tree with a wet sponge on the tip of a long cane. Any candle which showed signs of setting a branch alight was immediately extinguished. On arrival each child was handed a poke containing six buns or cakes and had his cup filled to the brim with tea which came in never-ending abundance. Indeed, the boys vied with one another to drink the greatest number of cups. Ushered later to file round the tree, we were each handed an apple and an orange and the present of some toy or game. The local gentry were very open-handed in their gifts to the Christmas Tree, as they also were in supplying books as prizes at the annual prizegiving in June.

It is said that old men forget. Ah. No! They remember and oft with advantages. Many of the folk and events of our childhood and youth do not fade but linger on. They form a large part of our personal history and, added one story to another, become the story of a village or a parish. Perhaps I may set down some of my memories.

I was born in 1912, on an auspicious day, Victoria Day, the 24th of May, still called then by older folk, the Auld Queen's Birthday, though she had been dead more than a decade. Scots were patriotic then and had a real pride in the Empire and all it stood for. The Great War took its toll of patriotism and loyalty; the second Great War has completed their erosion.

Once a year we were assembled in the playground around the great flagstaff which dominated it. The Union Jack was hoisted to the masthead and we were treated to an inspiring speech fron one or another of the local notables. The flagstaff is long gone, now, but in our day it served more than one purpose. It had four strong stays of plaited wire which splayed out to the four corners of the concrete platform on which it stood. We invented a game called "Change a Sixpence" which consisted of a rapid exchange from one corner to its opposite number, in the face of sturdy opposition. We enjoyed all the normal seasonal games of Scots children, 'bools' or marbles in the Spring and chestnut contests in the Autumn. The girls had their own games, 'ba'-beds' and 'peevers', and endless varieties of skipping-ropes, either singly or with two lasses ca'ing the ropes, and as many as half a dozen leaping through the ropes. In Winter, there was sledging on the Balloch Brae, for cars were almost non-existent then, or in the Laggan Park. Later we took to skating at Muirend Pond or at the House of Ross. There were endless games of Cowboys and Indians, or Romans and Britons in the Craig o' Ross wood, taking great care, of course, to avoid stepping on the Devil's Footprint on the top of the rock.

Our headmaster was Mr James Goldie, in my opinion the last of the old-style village dominies. He might well have been the prototype of the rhyme, "Comrie School's a good school, it's made o' lime and plaster, the only thing that's wrong wi' it, is the baldy-heided Master." Mr Goldie was quite devoid of hair.

Another great event of the school year was the School concert in June. The Public Hall would be crowded to capacity with adoring parents and all the local big-wigs seated on comfortable chairs in the front rows while the vulgar throng made do on hard, resisting benches. Mr Goldie came into his element then as he was something of a musician and well able to train infant voices. Many of the choruses he wrote himself and some have stayed with me after a fair lifetime.

There was the Eskimo Song, sung by twelve wee laddies clothed in saffron smocks of their mothers' making -

> We are twelve little Esquimaux and we
> come from the fields of snow
> We laugh with glee, Ha, Ha, Hee, Hee,
> and we never any taller grow.

The last statement was proved incorrect some four years later when the song was revived having the same performers. The smocks had shrunk or we had grown and considerable areas of leg and arm were now exposed, while buttons would no longer fit buttonholes.

We sang the patriotic verses for these were the dark days of the First World War:

> Our Daddy's dressed in Khaki,
> he's gone away to fight,
> For King and Home and Country,
> for Honour and for Right.

> We do not want the Germans
> to come all over here,
> So Dad must go and fight them,
> he'll beat them, never fear.

> So here's three cheers for Daddy,
> We would not wish him back,
> For we are little Britons,
> and love the Union Jack.

Who can forget, wee Willie McIntyre, perspiring profusely in his kilt, velvet jacket and starched collar as he recited, annually by popular demand, "'Twas a rat, 'twas a moose, 'twas a rat," or the bonnie lassies who sang "The Rowan Tree" and danced the Shean Trubhais?

There was scarcely a bairn in Comrie School when I joined the class in 1917 who did not have a father, brother or uncle far away in France. The burden on the womenfolk was enormous as they strove to keep us fed and decent on the pitifully small allotments of soldiers' pay. Our nation owes as great a debt to the women of our land as to their soldier husbands, who, all too often, never returned. One can learn of the enormity of Comrie's sacrifice from that wonder-

204

ful compilation, "Comrie War Book", published by that organising genius Sandy McGregor. Sandy it was who in 1924 was responsible for the management of the Muckle Merkat held in the Killing Hoose Park at the station, which raised the money for buying uniforms and instruments for the new pipe band, and for years thereafter the annual Pipe Band contests. Things went like clockwork, it seemed, even the weather being under Sandy's control, so much so that we knew that on Games Day we should be favoured with McGreegor's cloudless skies. It was at the Muckle Merkat that I first heard the "wireless" for the price of a threepenny bit.

The first time I saw the cinema, if I may grace it with such a grand name, was in Kemp's Park, sitting on hard wooden benches in a tent. It was called Bingo's Cinema, if I remember aright. Kemp's Park was the annual venue of tiny circuses and their sideshows, with their flaring Naphtha lamps and the wonderful steam organs. You got a lot for a penny in those days!

A weekly cinema came to Comrie in the Public Hall, under the auspices of Alf Clark, to be followed by Bob Crerar and his brother, Danny. Peter Crerar of Crieff, that great entrepreneur, followed them with the "Talkies" about 1929.

The buses came to Comrie in the shape of "Stoorie Aggie", a wooden box on wheels, run, I think, by a gentleman named Tainsh. A competitor soon followed in the shape of Holden's Motors with a charabanc type of vehicle, again to be succeeded by Peter Crerar's comfortable vehicles. Another great event was when Crerar brought the Queen of Loch Earn through the village and she just scraped through under the railway bridge by the old U.P. Kirk. She continued to sail up and down the loch from St Fillans to Lochearnhead for several years, a brave sight, particularly when viewed from the hill tops around.

The Comrie of fifty/sixty years ago was a far livelier place than it is today, in many respects. There was

Changing times

much more movement in the countryside. Motorcars were few and far between and most folks walked or cycled. On Sunday afternoons family groups took to the roads and pathways. There was so much more to see at a gentle and leisurely pace; time to look at wild flowers and listen to the birds sing. Where is now the wonderful 'dawn chorus' of yesteryear? Today we have but a pale echo of what we once knew. When did we last hear that disturber of the warm summer nights, the corncrake? The whaups and the lapwings are now banished to the glens. And where are all the bonnie wee birds, the whin chats and stone chats, the warblers and the scotch canaries? For every one that we see today there were dozens when we were laddies.

And too, we might ask, where have all the folk gone who lived their busy lives here. Every farm around had its quota of horsemen and cattlemen and their wives and bairns. Dunira estate in its heyday gave direct employment to a hundred people – made up of some two dozen house staff, two dozen gardeners, foresters, chauffeurs, gamekeepers, farm hands, electricians, joiners and builders. Many 'big hooses' employed three and four gardeners and as many indoor servants. Now all this is gone. There has been a whole silent revolution going on during our lifetimes, so silent that we are only aware of it after it has happened. The Clearances have been a continuing process.

Where, too, have all the small tradesmen gone who made their living here, for Comrie, at the beginning of the century was still the self-contained place it had been for two centuries past? We had two blacksmiths, three coal merchants, four or five bakers, each baking on their own premises, three cobblers and shoemakers, several tailors and outfitters. Gradually, all their work has disappeared into the maws of the city multiples.

In those now seeming far-off days, the farms were worked with pairs of horses. Every biggish place had two or three pairs of such handsome beasts. Farmtouns seemed much busier and thranger places than they do now, with their great stacks of hay and oats. Somehow they had a feeling of warmth and comfort and well-being which are now gone. They were weel-stackit and theekit, their place being taken by a bleak silo and bales all stowed away in sheds or confined within black plastic bags. The annual arrival of the travelling threshing mill was a thrill not to be missed. It always came in the early autumn dark and with its swinging lanterns, its flashes of fire from the firebox, and the sparks and smoke from the chimney, it seemed, indeed, like some prehistoric monster as it thundered and swayed up the brae to Craggish. Little did we know of the long tiring hours of back-breaking effort that waited the folks of the farm on the morrow.

How pleasant to remember the annual ploughing matches in Comrie and at Monzievaird! How we used to dash away from school at four o'clock to be in at the finish. There is nothing that begins to compare with the sight of a dozen or more well-matched pairs of great Clydesdales, effortlessly drawing a furrow. What odd prizes there were in addition to those for ploughing skills! There was one for the oldest ploughman, for the man first on the field, for the man coming the longest distance, for the best-looking ploughman, for the man with the largest family, and so on. One prize I remember, was a shirt from Peter Macpherson's, price 7s.6d. No one went empty away. And then there was always the chance of a 'hurl' home on somebody's cart. A tractor and bogie do not begin to compare.

These, too, were the great days of the grouse-driving on the moors – the 'beating' as we called it. Come the Glorious Twelfth and perhaps forty or fifty or more laddies would be trysted to turn up at Pate Macpherson's, come rain or shine, at eight o'clock in the morning, and be driven in Charlie Richard's charabanc, or Keithy Macpherson's Austin taxi or with Bill Drummond at the wheel of the great Studebaker, crammed in like herrings in a barrel, a merry throng. Twenty miles and more would we tramp over heather and rock, under the benevolent eye of Tam Doo of Carroglen, Joe Wilson at Invergeldie, hardy Sandy Campbell at Lochside, Archie Cameron at Aberuchill, and all for the princely sum of six shillings a day. Our contract, so to say, was with the head gamekeeper and we had little to do with the 'guns' or 'toffs' as we called them. Some of them, I'm afraid did consider us beneath their notice. Indeed, one of them, Col. Courage, who had recently bought Invergeldie, a man of vast wealth, whose name appeared over half the public houses of Southern England, canvassed the other lairds, hoping to reduce our pittance to four shillings a day. He met with a stony rebuff and was never to our knowledge, invited elsewhere to a day's shooting. On one occasion he deigned to speak to the late Jock McNab, whose father had a garage business in Comrie, with the words, "I suppose those chaps will be on the dole when the shooting stops." "Indeed, no" said Jock, "you don't realise it, but seven of these twenty youths are University graduates on holiday." It was a great life, hard, yes, but healthy. In the course of the season we would destroy a pair of boots and a suit of clothes, but that's what the various six shillings replaced. In the hungry twenties and thirties, we were all poor, and when all are poor, none are rich. We were rich in the things that mattered.

Who does not recall the concert parties which used to come to the Public Hall? They came, usually, from Glasgow and Edinburgh and brought with them a whiff, not always welcome, of the wider world. Do you remember Mr McLean, the dancing-master, who taught or tried to teach us dancing? How light he was on his feet as he skipped around with his fiddle under his chin! Long-remembered are the Christmas Tree parties and the Sunday School Soirees. Do you recall Mr Alec Peggie, the Auld Kirk organist, and his stirring musical, Rob Roy? and Mr Jim Rowe of the Free Kirk with his cantatas? There was never a week in Winter when some form of wholesome entertainment was not laid on, mostly by local effort, kitchen comedies and kailyaird sketches. Then there were Band of Hope meetings taken by the Rev. Mr Watt and limelight lectures on many subjects. From one of these on Mary Queen of Scots, I conceived and long maintained a powerful dislike of her mother, Mary of Guise, whom I now realise to have been a sorely tried lady who was thwarted at every turn by John Knox and his fellow presbyters.

Every possible interest of young people was catered for in the Comrie of my childhood and youth. In summer we could fish for 'baggie-minnows' in the Ruchill with a worm on a bent pin and 'dook' at the 'Tent Linn'. We often went to school in June in our bare feet sand-shoes had scarcely been invented then. We would wade across the Earn below the Ross Brig in the shallows beyond the 'Ivy Hole', always trying to avoid the 'eelie' beds lest we step on an eel and cut our feet on their tails – such was our belief.

We had the 21st Perthshire Boy Scout Troop run by Miss Florence Graham-Stirling of Camp Cottage and the Cubs. The girls had the S.G.F.S., the Scots Girls Friendly Society, the Guides and the Brownies. Older lads and young men had football in the Laggan Park - Comrie Rovers, the Violet and even a very junior team, the Victoria. There were two putting greens, a tennis court, bowling green and a quoiting pitch; there was golf and the angling club. This was, indeed, a busy wee place and much interest was added to it by the great numbers of holiday folk who took rooms here in the summertime. There was hardly a house here but had its quota of city-dwellers either 'with attendance' or 'with full board'. I have even known a henhouse to be pressed into service. The railway had put Comrie on the map.

And who were the folk that I remember with affection from these, now far-off days. There was Tommy Stirling, farm manager at Craggish, a dapper fellow in tight knee breeches and loudly checked jacket and cap. He always had his "morning" around 11 o'clock and would return on his motor-bike about mid-day. As often as not the primitive machine would give up the ghost near our home. Tommy would step off and deliver one or two heavy kicks to the machine, push it off, and believe it or not, the thing would start again. It was to Craggish that the travelling threshing mill would come in the darkness, having finished at some farm in the late afternoon. It seemed a great prehistoric monster as it passed, hissing steam and emitting clouds of smoke. A combine harvester is a gentle well-behaved giant by comparison. There was something alive and vital about the steam traction engine. It spoke of power and energy.

At the head of the Ross lived the Morrisons who are said to have farmed on Aberuchill at Old Craggish for 300 years. Sandy Morrison died before my time, leaving two sisters and some memories. He was a devout elder of the Free Kirk. He would not dream of working on the Sabbath. The very idea of yoking a horse on the Lord's Day was not to be thought of. Still, when the Free Kirk decided to install a "kist o' whistles" during Johnnie Graham's time, Sandy lifted his lines, yoked the horse to the cart and drove to the kirk in St Fillans. In avoiding one of Satan's traps, he fell into another. The Deil's a clever fellow! The Morrisons had two nephews with whom, though they were a bit older than I, I had friendship throughout their lives. They told me that evening worship was regular in the Morrison home and when they were on holiday there, it was expected that the boys would read a passage at random, wherever the good Book happened to fall open. Knowing that the old folk were quite fond of their nightly mutchkin, the boys arranged that the Book should fall open at Proverbs 20, Verse 1 which reads, "wine is a mocker, strong drink is raging and whoever is deceived thereby is not wise." That was the end of holiday time readings.

Our immediate neighbour was Geordie Quack-quack, otherwise Geordie Retson. He was a specialist to trade, a molecatcher. His great dream in life was to catch enough white, albino moles, as would make his wife a white moleskin coat. He never made it but he made my Mother a present of one white moleskin, so I can vouch that there are such things. Geordie smoked a pipe and was the only man I remember who did not use matches. He always used flint, steel and tinder-paper. These articles he kept in the same pocket along with his tin of strychnine for poisoning moles. The wonder is that he lived to be an old man - a real rough diamond.

At Castle Folly lived Thunder Jock McNaughton, a carter, who, when his horse bogged down on one occasion, took the horse from the shafts and put himself in its place. As he said afterwards, "I dinna wonder the horse got stuck, I nearly got stuck masel!". His neighbour was old Will McRostie, a retired farmer of whom I was mortally afraid. He was forever threatening to put my wee sister in a big black poke. In Balmoral Cottage lived the McLarens. Old Will McLaren used to cut my hair as I sat in his front garden, literally with a bowl on my head. You will have heard of a bowl-clip, I have no doubt. Quite a change from modern styling!

Then there were John and Mrs Strachan in the market garden. Many a pennyworth of yellow sulphur gooseberries we gathered for ourselves in his garden. He would always say, after taking our pennies, just keep whistling. This was easily done as we never went singly. John was fairly fond of his dram. One night my father who was a staunch Good Templar, came on Johnnie making his way over the Ross Brig with some difficulty. Having assisted Johnnie to his door, my father left him there and went on his way home to be followed by loud cries of, "Will ye be a' richt noo, Davie? Will ye manage hame?"

As children we had the free run of the fields and woods of the House of Ross. The McLagans liked to hear the sound of children's voices. Many a winter's evening by the light of the moon we spent sliding and skating on the pond. It was here on the braes that we rolled our Easter Eggs and fed hay to the old horse, Barbara, who had been wounded in the Boer War and lived to be over thirty. We knew where the old-time volunteers used to fire their heavy lead bullets into the rock. These we would pick out with a knife and make sinkers for our fishing casts. The best chestnuts in the Ross came from a tree in front of Drumearn House. Sadly the years have taken the tree away, and the old walnut tree behind the wall has gone, too. We used to come home like Red Indians stained by the juice of the pulpy covering of the shells.

Such then was the Comrie we knew when I was young, three quarters of a century ago. It is now a much changed place but is yet a bonnie dwelling-place. Much that is part and parcel of the remaining Comrie folk will pass with them. How long will it be before the real tones and accents of Comrie are heard no more? I do not give it another decade. There was something cosy and couthy about the tongue of the folk of my youth which I am beginning to miss, more and more. As far as Comrie is concerned, the Gaelic of our forefathers is no more. My Granny had the Gaelic. I have none, and I think that a great loss. The commonly used Lowland Scots of my childhood is rapidly disappearing before the onslaught of the BBC, and heaven help us, even their English is being prostituted by outside influences, mainly Transatlantic. Why should we believe that a form of English as received and spoken in the neighbourhood of London is superior to our Lowland Scots, which is merely another form of English, but I venture to say, very much more expressive and kindly?

Who can forget the old nick-names of Comrie, for we all had nick-names, even if we were not aware of them? Who was Half a banana, Pate the Bully, Jimmy the Brat, and Jimmie Dookie, Camsauch and Trottin' Johnnie, Jumpin' Jimmy and Saut and Barley? Surely these were names to be remembered with as much affection as Tam o'Shanter and Soutar Johnnie!

Where is Muirend Curling Pond and where and why, in the Ross, the Sawdust Road and the Bog? What is their origin and why were they so named? Where is the Ark and where the Plane Tree, the Bulwarks and the Ladies' Linn? Where is the Drum and where the Coach Turn? They are marked on no map but exist in folk-memory. Do we still call a thrush a mavie, a chaffinch a jink, and a sparrow a speug? Is a curlew still a whaup, an oyster catcher a pleep, and a lapwing a peesweep?

It may seem in the broad sweep of things and events that these are but small matters. I venture to say that this is not so. They are all of the pith and marrow of our being. And if these things are not our story, then I do not know what they are.

This, then, is the story of a fairly long life. Much, very much has had to be left out. It is good to recall the kindly folk we have known in Auld Lang Syne. All this has passed into our personal history. These folk, these events, these happenings went, each of them, into the history of our village. For all that happens today is the history of tomorrow. None of these things can ever happen again, either in the same way, or at all. They should be brought to mind as they mark the history of our lifetime.

INDEX

216